NAVIGATING HYBRID SCRUM ENVIRONMENTS

UNDERSTANDING THE ESSENTIALS, AVOIDING THE PITFALLS

Frederik M. Fowler

Apress®

Navigating Hybrid Scrum Environments: Understanding the Essentials,
Avoiding the Pitfalls

Frederik M. Fowler
Sunnyvale, CA
USA

ISBN-13 (pbk): 978-1-4842-4163-9   ISBN-13 (electronic): 978-1-4842-4164-6
https://doi.org/10.1007/978-1-4842-4164-6

Library of Congress Control Number: 2018962960

Managing Director, Apress Media LLC: Welmoed Spahr
Acquisitions Editor: Shiva Ramachandran
Development Editor: Laura Berendson
Coordinating Editor: Rita Fernando

Cover designed by eStudioCalamar

Distributed to the book trade worldwide by Springer Science+Business Media New York, 233 Spring Street, 6th Floor, New York, NY 10013. Phone 1-800-SPRINGER, fax (201) 348-4505, e-mail orders-ny@springer-sbm.com, or visit www.springeronline.com. Apress Media, LLC is a California LLC and the sole member (owner) is Springer Science + Business Media Finance Inc (SSBM Finance Inc). SSBM Finance Inc is a **Delaware** corporation.

For information on translations, please e-mail rights@apress.com, or visit http://www.apress.com/rights-permissions.

Apress titles may be purchased in bulk for academic, corporate, or promotional use. eBook versions and licenses are also available for most titles. For more information, reference our Print and eBook Bulk Sales web page at http://www.apress.com/bulk-sales.

Any source code or other supplementary material referenced by the author in this book is available to readers on GitHub via the book's product page, located at www.apress.com/9781484241639. For more detailed information, please visit http://www.apress.com/source-code.

Printed on acid-free paper

For my best friend, George S. Berry, who taught me never to be afraid to try new things. R. I. P.

Contents

About the Author.. vii

Acknowledgments ix

Introduction: The "Why" Part of Scrum xi

Part I: The Overall Approach Behind Scrum 1

Chapter 1:   What Is Scrum? 3

Chapter 2:   Scrum Theory.....................................9

Chapter 3:   Scrum and Waterfall 13

**Part II: The Components of Scrum: The Scrum
             Roles 23**

Chapter 4:   The Scrum Team 25

Chapter 5:   Scrum Team Roles 31

Chapter 6:   The Scrum Development Team 39

Chapter 7:   The Scrum Master.................................47

**Part III: The Components of Scrum: The Scrum
             Artifacts 53**

Chapter 8:   Scrum Artifacts 55

Chapter 9:   The Product Backlog...............................59

Chapter 10: The Sprint Backlog 67

**Part IV: The Components of Scrum: The Scrum
             Events 71**

Chapter 11: Scrum Events.....................................73

Chapter 12: The Sprint.......................................77

Chapter 13: The Sprint Planning Meeting 83

Chapter 14: The Daily Scrum 89

Chapter 15: The Sprint Review 93

Chapter 16: The Sprint Retrospective 97

Part V: Conclusion 101

Chapter 17: Conclusion 103

Appendix A: Scrum for Projects. 107

Appendix B: Scaled Scrum 111

Appendix C: Scrum for the Program and Portfolio Levels 117

Index 121

About the Author

Frederik M. Fowler has been developing software in Silicon Valley for more than 35 years and has been using the Scrum Framework since 2006. He is one of only about 50 individuals in the United States who holds the prestigious "Professional Scrum Master level III" (PSM III) certification awarded by Scrum.org. In 2013, Fred left his post as vice-president and Chief Information Officer of a Silicon Valley 150 company to devote his time to teaching and coaching Scrum/Agile. Since then, he has helped both start-ups, not-for-profits and Fortune 500 organizations, teaching more than 300 people in the United States, India, China, and Central America. More information is available at www.SiliconValleyScrum.com.

Acknowledgments

I thank Phyllis Keene Fowler, my wife of 38 years and my first and best editor, for her many contributions to this work.

I also thank my friend and fellow author Larry Apke for the many conversations we've had that helped me develop and refine the ideas expressed in this book.

Introduction: The "Why" Part of Scrum

"... when faced with a problem you do not understand, do any part of it that you do understand, then look at it again."

—Robert Heinlein, *The Moon is a Harsh Mistress* (1966)

Some years ago it became fashionable for managers to make light of their staff's questions by asking, "What part of NO don't you understand?" This catch phrase lasted until savvy people developed a pat answer. When asked "What part of NO don't you understand?" smart people soon started to reply "the WHY part."

Understanding the "why" part of anything is usually the key to mastering that thing. This is especially true of the Scrum Framework.

Developed by Ken Schwaber and Jeff Sutherland, the Scrum Framework has revolutionized the solving of complex problems for those who have mastered it. When applied in the field of software development, Scrum results in astounding improvements in product quality, developer productivity, and time-to-market speed.

As described by Schwaber and Sutherland in *The Scrum Guide*,[1] Scrum is lightweight, simple to understand, difficult to master. Scrum presents a framework of simple roles, artifacts, and events that can be applied in any situation in which there is more that is not known about a problem than there is that is known. Scrum organizes activities into processes in which results are discovered rather than predicted. The net effect is to allow everyone involved to focus on the correct tasks at the correct times to produce superior outcomes quickly and efficiently.

---

[1]Ken Schwaber and Jeff Sutherland. *The Scrum Guide*, *http://www.ScrumGuides.org*, November 2017.

The Scrum Framework itself is magnificently simple and elegant. As housed in *The Scrum Guide*, the entire Scrum body of knowledge is only 19 pages long. There are three roles (Product Owner, Developer, and Scrum Master), three artifacts (Product Backlog, Sprint Backlog and Sprint Increment), and five events (Sprint, Sprint Planning Meeting, Daily Scrum, Sprint Review and Sprint Retrospective). The entirety of the Scrum Framework can be reviewed in a matter of minutes.

Learning to apply the Scrum Framework, however, can take much longer.

Someone with a traditional project management background will find parts of Scrum to be familiar and parts of it to be a little strange. The idea of daily "stand-up" meetings is easily grasped as a form of status reporting. Organizing work into sprints with periodic "demo" events is easily "recognized" as a milestone tracking mechanism. These two parts of the Scrum Framework are usually the first ones to be implemented by a non-Scrum shop that wants to become "scrummy."

Other parts of the Scrum Framework present more of a challenge to the credulity of a traditional project management professional. Requiring that teams of developers manage themselves can seem like a utopian counterculture fantasy. Embarking on a major software development project without a concrete plan seems like folly. Having a "Scrum master" instead of a project manager makes little sense, especially when this "master" turns out to be a servant leader who is the master of no one.

The Scrum Framework was created by hard-headed realists who understood how software is created in the real world. Every part of it depends on every other part. As the authors of *The Scrum Guide* state within it, it is possible to "pick and choose" among the elements of Scrum, but the result will not be Scrum unless the framework is embraced and adopted in its entirety.

There is a hard-headed, practical reason for including every component of the Scrum Framework. Even the ones that seem strange and/or radical have a reason for being part of it. Leaving bits and pieces out of the mix will have adverse consequences.

There are plenty of books on the general subject of "How Scrum Works." Many sources are available to describe the three roles, three artifacts, and five events.

This book explains "Why Scrum Works." It explains why there are three roles, why there are three artifacts, and why there are five events. It sheds light on the reasons behind the Scrum Framework's characteristics, especially the strange and controversial ones, so that adopters can avoid the temptation to pick and choose.

Each characteristic of the Scrum Framework serves a purpose. This book explains what those purposes are.

Only by understanding the purposes behind each part of the Scrum Framework can rational choices be made about customizing it. If one part of the Framework is dropped, something else should be put in place to serve the underlying purpose behind it.

The Scrum Framework is magnificently simple, yet its scope is profound. My hope is that the work of Ken Schwaber and Jeff Sutherland will come into clearer focus when practitioners understand not only "how" but "why" Scrum works.

The Overall Approach Behind Scrum

What Is Scrum?

I have been engaged in software development for more than 35 years. I have written code for organizations both big and small. I have created both individual programs and entire software systems to address business problems of all kinds. I have worked as a solo developer and as part of large teams. Over the course of my career, I have learned quite a bit about how software development works.

I've come to realize that certain values and principles make a great deal of sense when it comes to organizing a software development effort. There are certain truths I have discovered that I now consider to be self-evident:

- That software is always created by technicians to fill the real-world needs of less-technical people

- That software producers and users must work together on a daily basis to produce valuable results

- That both technical and nontechnical people must interact in an atmosphere of mutual respect and trust

- That the best way for these people to interact is by examining actual functionality that has been produced, and by continuously refining that functionality as both the technical and nontechnical people learn more about the problems they are solving

These self-evident truths are nothing original or new. They are, in fact, some of the values and principles documented in the *Manifesto for Agile Software*

© Frederik M. Fowler 2019
F. M. Fowler, *Navigating Hybrid Scrum Environments*,
https://doi.org/10.1007/978-1-4842-4164-6_1

Development, commonly known as the "Agile Manifesto." (The Manifesto can be found at www.agilemanifesto.org). This Manifesto was created in February 2001 as a joint effort by 17 prominent software developers. Their goal was to identify and document their common findings behind a number of (then) new approaches to "lightweight" software development.

It is very important to realize that the Agile Manifesto was not created by a group of theoreticians locked up in an ivory tower. The very first sentence in the Manifesto states:

> *"We are uncovering better ways of developing software by doing it and helping others do it ...."*

In other words, the manifesto was created by hard-headed realists who had "been through the wars" and had learned through tough experience how important the values and principles of the Agile Manifesto are.

Two of those original 17 people were Jeff Sutherland and Ken Schwaber, the creators of the Scrum Framework. They had originally described Scrum six years earlier at a conference called "Object-Oriented Programming, Systems, Languages & Applications '95." Many of the values and principals in the Agile Manifesto come from the earlier work of Sutherland and Schwaber presented at the conference.

The definition of the Scrum Framework can be found in *The Scrum Guide*, coauthored by Sutherland and Schwaber, and at the time of this writing is available online at www.scrumguides.org. *The Scrum Guide* outlines a framework for implementing many of the Agile Manifesto's values and principles.

Lots of people these days have asked me, "What is the difference between Agile and Scrum?" Many people seem to think that "Agile methodologies" and "Scrum methodologies" are distinct alternatives to each other. They seem to think that organizations may be "Agile" or "Scrum" but not both.

The truth is that comparing Agile and Scrum in this way makes no sense at all. "Agile" is an abstract set of values and principals described in the Agile Manifesto. "Scrum" is a concrete framework described in *The Scrum Guide* for organizing the creation of products. Agile and Scrum are related in that Scrum is a concrete implementation of the abstract values and principals described in the Agile Manifesto.

The Scrum Framework has been one of the most successful innovations in software development practice since software development first became a profession. When implemented properly, the Scrum Framework produces truly breathtaking improvements in productivity and the ability of organizations to deliver value.

Many organizations have noted these improvements and wish to embrace the Scrum Framework. Unfortunately, they often try to implement the Scrum

Framework without truly understanding what it is. They end up implementing those parts of it that they feel they recognize and understand. They often leave out other parts of the framework that seem "strange" and "against common sense." The results are usually disappointing for everyone involved.

As noted in *The Scrum Guide*, Scrum is

- Lightweight
- Easy to understand
- Difficult to master

Scrum is lightweight in that it can be defined in a short and concise document. *The Scrum Guide* is only 19 pages long. Other frameworks such as the Project Management Institute's (PMI) *Project Management Body of Knowledge* (PMBOK) require hundreds of pages to describe. *The Scrum Guide* boils the framework down into just 11 elegant concepts (three "roles," three "artifacts," and five "events").

Scrum is easy to understand in that it can be explained in a classroom setting in about 16 hours of class time. During any given month, there are dozens of two-day class sessions being held all over the world. These classes prepare people to take and pass "Scrum Master Certification" examinations.

As lightweight and as easy to understand as Scrum is, it turns out to be truly difficult to master. It is difficult because the Scrum Framework requires us to use measurements to understand the realities of software development. When we use these measurements to show us these realities, the truth usually conflicts with our notion of what "common sense" tells us. The Scrum Framework shows us how software development really works. In effect, the Scrum Framework forces us to confront many false ideas we have all taken for granted for a long time. Mastering Scrum involves "unlearning" many false lessons we have learned over the years.

The Definition of Scrum

The Scrum Guide contains a concise definition of the word *Scrum*:

> *Scrum (n): A framework within which people can address complex adaptive problems, while productively and creatively delivering products of the highest possible value.*

There are three important aspects of Scrum that this definition makes clear. The first one is that the Scrum Framework is focused on delivering *value*. The Scrum Framework is not about increasing productivity or making the software development process more efficient. The purpose of the Scrum Framework is to maximize value through the delivery of valuable products. Please note that the definition of Scrum does not refer only to *software* products. Scrum is meant to be applicable to the creation of *any* kind of product.

The second important aspect of the Scrum definition is that Scrum is not appropriate for solving *all* kinds of problems. Scrum is designed specifically to solve *complex adaptive* problems. There are many kinds of problems in the world that Scrum is poorly adapted to address. As we will see, there are other frameworks that are better suited to address both simple and complicated challenges. It is only when problems become complex that the Scrum Framework becomes applicable.

The third aspect of Scrum that the definition makes clear is that Scrum is a *framework*. Many people mistakenly believe that Scrum is a "methodology" or a set of "procedures." The Scrum Framework is made up of eleven components organized into three families. One family (the events) contains five components that are all procedures. These procedures are the most "visible" parts of the Scrum Framework and are often the parts of Scrum that are implemented first. If they are the only parts of Scrum that are implemented, however, the results are usually quite bad. If the nonprocedural parts of Scrum are left out, then the procedures often make things worse rather than better.

Methodologies and Frameworks

Methodologies are families of methods, and methods are procedural ways of producing desired results. We are all very familiar with using and following procedures in our daily lives. As we will see, procedures are good and useful ways of addressing both simple and complicated problems.

A procedure is a step-by-step plan for producing a desired result. A very good example of a procedure is a recipe. If someone is hungry and wants to have a waffle, there is a recipe that can be followed to produce one. The steps are (1) to assemble the ingredients, (2) to mix them together in their proper proportions to make a batter, (3) to preheat the waffle iron, and (4) to bake the batter in the waffle iron until the waffle is ready to eat.

A framework is not a procedure. It is not meant to produce desired results. A framework is a tool used to arrange and organize things according to a set of desired relationships. A framework identifies the relationships between its components and, as such, it controls the ways in which its components interact.

A methodology is about doing things. A framework, however, is about organizing things. The Scrum Framework's primary function is to organize people and their relationships into an effective structure. After the people are organized, the Scrum Framework gives them tools and procedures to use to measure and manage their work.

People who are organized properly can use the tools and procedures within Scrum to achieve breathtaking results. If they are not organized according to the Scrum Framework, the Scrum tools and procedures are of little help and often cause more harm than good. Most companies that adopt the procedural aspects of Scrum without accepting the organizational aspects of it are doomed to frustration and failure. Only those organizations that implement the complete Scrum Framework can expect to reap its benefits.

Complex Problems

Problems can be grouped together into families depending on their characteristics. "Complex adaptive" problems are challenges containing many aspects that are not yet known or understood. Solving a complex adaptive problem involves finding and understanding those unknown factors. The process of addressing a complex adaptive problem involves a process of discovery. Solutions are discovered rather than implemented.

A "complicated" problem, on the other hand, does not contain unknown factors. The solution may be intricate, but in the end everything needed to solve the problem is known at the outset.

To understand the difference, let's consider an example. Let's suppose that we are home builders and that we have just acquired a large piece of land. We plan to build 100 identical houses on that parcel. After a bit of preparation, we get to work.

When the time comes to build the 99th house, is there very much that is unknown about how to build it? No, not at all.

By the time we're constructing the 99th house, we have 98 houses worth of experience teaching us how to build number 99. We know exactly how many 2 × 4 boards are needed, how many nails, how much plumbing pipe, and how many workers are required. The 99th house is a "complicated" problem in that there are many different components that are required. There is very little that is unknown at that point, however. It is possible to create a detailed plan (or a recipe) that will produce the house we want to build.

The 99th house is a "complicated" problem, but how about the first house?

When we are building the first house, we have no direct experience we can use to predict all the challenges we will encounter. When building the first house, we will find all the things we didn't anticipate or understand properly when we got started. We may discover, for instance, that we placed the master bathroom on the second floor above the dining room on the first floor, so that dinner guests will hear the toilet flushing above them while they are eating. We may discover that not enough clearance has been left for the staircase, so that people hit their head on the ceiling while going upstairs. We may find that we've left too much distance between the hot-water heater and the upstairs bathroom shower, letting the hot water lose all of its heat before reaching its destination.

Building the first house is a "complex" problem. There are many aspects of building the house that are unknown and that cannot be known until we actually build it. The way to proceed is to start building and deal with any unexpected challenges as we go. As we encounter unanticipated challenges, we solve them and then update our master plan so that we won't be hindered by them when building the next house.

Software Development Is a Complex Problem

To what extent is software development a "complex" problem? The answer has to do with whether developing software is more like building the 99th house or the first house in our homebuilding example.

The process of creating anything for the first time involves finding and solving unexpected problems. Software developers almost always run into such challenges.

In our homebuilding example, every time an unanticipated complication is encountered, the master plan is updated so the issue will not get in the way the next time a house is built.

For software, however, there is no "next time."

After software has been written, there is no need to write it again. There is no second or third (or 99th) copy to write. In effect, developing software is always like building that first house in the set. Writing software always involves dealing with unexpected challenges, because once software is written, there is no need ever to write it again the same way.

By the way, the same can be said for developing *any* kind of new product, regardless of whether it is a software product. New products, by definition, have never been created before. This means that developing them requires finding and solving many unknown challenges. After those challenges have been overcome, there is no need to update any "master plan." After a product has been developed, there is no need to develop it the same way again.

Summary

Scrum is a framework that facilitates an organized process of discovery. It organizes people into teams that can discover and deal with the unexpected. They learn as they go. In the end, they create products by discovering solutions to the unexpected challenges they encounter on their way to delivering the desired result.

Scrum Theory

The Scrum Framework is built on an extensive theoretical base that ranges from systems analytics to team interactions and human behavior. Ken Schwaber and Jeff Sutherland put the pieces together during the 1990s, but its theoretical roots go back to at least the 1980s and, arguably, back to the 1950s as well.

Scrum's organizational aspects are based on the work of Hirotaka Takeuchi and Ikujiro Nonaka, two Japanese academics who studied teamwork at the Toyota Motor Company. They published their findings in 1986.[1] These two scholars were the first to use the word *Scrum* to describe team behavior. Their observations at Toyota reminded them of a play in rugby football. During the rugby "scrum" each team huddles together in a big cluster to push the ball forward. This idea of "the whole team pushing together" is what Takeuchi and Nonaka found to be the most compelling aspect of the way effective teams worked together at Toyota.

Scrum's artifacts and events are based on the theory of Empirical Process Control. This theory draws on the work of W. Edwards Deming and others; it holds that decisions should be made based on measurements of actual facts as opposed to predictions of future results. Empirical Process Control holds that it is impossible to predict future events and outcomes with any degree

---

[1]Hirotaka Takeuchi and Ikujiro Nonaka, "The New New Product Development Game." https://hbr.org/1986/01/the-new-new-product-development-game.

© Frederik M. Fowler 2019
F. M. Fowler, *Navigating Hybrid Scrum Environments*,
https://doi.org/10.1007/978-1-4842-4164-6_2

of certainty. It is not possible to be certain about future realities until after they have taken place, not before. The past is real. The future is a mystery and predictions of it are only guesswork.

There are three core principals in the theory of Empirical Process Control. They are as follows:

- **Transparency:** In this context, transparency means that every aspect of a product and the work of developing it should be visible and accessible to everyone who is involved. In other words, everything about the product should be on the table in plain sight. There should be no secrets, and all that is known about the product and its development should be examinable by everyone who has a stake in the outcome.

- **Inspection:** If there is transparency, then the people involved with the product have a duty to examine that transparency on a regular basis. The product and the work being done on it need to be inspected formally on a regular schedule.

- **Adaptation:** If there is transparency and a product is being inspected, then there ought to be lessons that are learned as a result. The principle of adaptation turns the formal inspection of transparency into a feedback loop in which lessons are learned from examining observed facts.

The "Empirical" part of Empirical Process Control comes from the emphasis on using observations instead of predictions. It turns out that the three core principles encapsulate the scientific method used in experimental sciences. In physics or chemistry, when something is to be learned, an experiment is constructed to test a hypothesis. The experiment is designed to produce clear results (transparency), which are then observed (inspection) and used to confirm, disprove, or alter the hypothesis (adaptation).

The Scrum Framework uses this scientific method approach to deal with the unknowns that are inherent in complex adaptive problems. Large problems are broken down into smaller pieces, and a few high-priority pieces are then implemented. After that work is done, the entire problem is reevaluated based on lessons learned. A new set of high-priority pieces are then selected, the work of implementing then takes place, and the process repeats.

This "experimental" approach to software development gives rise to the most visible aspect of the Scrum Framework. With Scrum, work is divided into two- to four-week Sprints. Each sprint has its own "scope," or set of functionality to produce.

The reason for dividing work into discrete sprints is to have some real results to measure. After each sprint, there are some new pieces of empirical data to add to our knowledge of the problem we are solving. When one sprint ends, the next one begins. The first activity in the new sprint is to create a plan for what to do next. The new plan takes into account any lessons learned from the previous sprint.

When setting out to create a new product using the Scrum Framework, an overall goal is set. A sprint is then planned and executed to take the first step toward that goal. After that sprint is completed, the lessons learned are evaluated and a second step toward the goal is taken. We keep going in this step-by-step process until we decide it makes no sense to continue. As long as there is value in doing so, we keep on going.

How Effective Is the Scrum Framework?

The main reason that organizations are interested in adopting the Scrum Framework is that there is plenty of evidence that it works very well. There is a famous example of the relative benefits of using a Scrum approach instead of a traditional approach. The example is the Sentinel project undertaken by the FBI in the mid 2000s. To understand the project, it is necessary to understand its background.

In summer 2001, the Phoenix, AZ, office of the FBI took note of some suspicious activity. A number of young men from the Middle East were taking flying lessons. Phoenix has a school for learning to fly large commercial jets, and these people had enrolled. They were especially interested in learning how to fly jets in level flight. They didn't seem to care much about taking off or landing. The FBI watched these individuals for a while, but they then vanished. They were no longer in the Phoenix area.

They later turned up in Boston, where they boarded a number of airplanes at Boston's Logan International airport. The date was September 11, 2001. These people flew two of the jets into the Twin Towers of the World Trade Center in New York. Another jet crashed into the Pentagon in Washington, DC. The fourth jet crashed in Pennsylvania after the passengers realized what was happening, attacked the hijackers, and gave their lives downing the airplane. It was the worst terrorist attack in US history.

In the aftermath of the attack, a congressional inquiry was held. One of the observations was that while the Phoenix office of the FBI was watching these individuals, the Boston office of the FBI knew nothing about them. It was decided that never again should the United States be attacked, in part, because one office of the FBI had information that another one needed and did not have. There was to be a single database and repository to consolidate all of the FBI's information so that every office would have access to all information available, no matter what the source.

Thus, the Sentinel project was born. Congress appropriated $450 million to get the job done and set a deadline of two years. Lockheed-Martin, a famous defense contractor, was engaged to manage the project. Lockheed hired 200 developers and got to work,

Eighteen months later, Lockheed-Martin came back to the FBI to report progress. Unfortunately, there was not much tangible progress to report. Some functions were complete but most of the work was yet to be done. Lockheed-Martin asked for more time and more money.

As a tax payer, I'm very grateful to the FBI for what they did next. They told Lockheed-Martin, "You're fired." They then brought in some "agilists" who reorganized the effort using the Scrum Framework.

The first thing the agilists did was drop 180 of the 200 developers. They proceeded with only 20 of the original people that Lockheed-Martin had hired.

What was the result? Those agilists and the 20 developers *delivered the entire working product only five months later.* Twenty people had done in five months what 200 people had been unable to do in 18 months.

Some simple arithmetic shows how dramatic a difference the Scrum Framework made. Just using the number of developers as a gauge, those 20 people were ten times as effective as the original 200 people who were hired. That is a 1,000% improvement.

When the difference in elapsed time (5 months vs. 18 months) and other factors are taken into account, the effect of using the Scrum Framework works out to be a 1,500% improvement.

Is it any wonder that so many organizations are interested in adopting the Scrum Framework?

How could 20 people do what 200 people could not? The 20 people were working in an organized way, whereas the 200 people were working in a disorganized way. The difference was organizing the work using the Scrum Framework as opposed to the traditional "waterfall" approach. Choosing the correct framework for organizing a project can make a huge difference.

Summary

The Scrum Framework relies on two main bodies of theory. It uses the ideas of Hirotaka Takeuchi and Ikujiro Nonaka as the basis for its roles and teams. It uses the theory of Empirical Process Control to give those teams the tools they need to manage the work. The result is a way of organizing people that is simple and very effective.

Scrum and Waterfall

The Scrum Framework was developed as a reaction to some frustrating limitations found in the "traditional" way software development work is organized. The traditional framework is codified in the PMI's PMBOK and is commonly known as the *system development life cycle* (SDLC) or *waterfall.*

The SDLC framework envisions software development as a series of "projects." Each project has a beginning, a middle, and an end. Throughout the life of a product, there may be many projects that are used to change or enhance the product's functionality. Each project is a discrete activity with its own scope, its own goals, its own budget, and its own schedule. Each project is independent of every other project and has nothing necessarily in common with any other project other than the fact that several projects may enhance the same product.

Projects begin with a proposal that is then reviewed by an approving authority. The approvers may be high-level managers, an approval committee, or some other authority that makes budgetary decisions. The proposal includes a description of the new product or enhancement, a projected cost, a projected return on the proposed investment, and an estimated delivery date.

The approvers evaluate the proposal and consider both the potential return on the investment (ROI) and the risk that the return may not be realized. They check whether the proposal fits within the organization's overall business strategy, and they consider whether it makes sense to proceed with this proposal rather than others that may be being considered as well.

© Frederik M. Fowler 2019
F. M. Fowler, *Navigating Hybrid Scrum Environments,*
https://doi.org/10.1007/978-1-4842-4164-6_3

If the approval authority gives its consent, budget money is set aside to work the project, and a due date is set for delivery of the project's work product. (This is known as *Gate 0* in the SDLC.)

The next step is to do detailed analysis and design, and create a detailed work breakdown schedule, or WBS. The WBS is usually created by software architects and engineering leads and is a list of technical tasks to be performed according to a specific sequence. Other planning activities also take place, including producing such things as a risk analysis and a risk mitigation plan.

The tasks in the WBS are usually represented as a Gantt chart that shows a schedule for the completion of each task. Each task is assigned an estimated duration and is arranged in a sequence that displays the prior tasks that must be completed before work can begin on the subsequent tasks dependent on them. Dependent tasks tend to form "chains" within the Gantt chart, with the longest chain called the *critical path* because its duration governs the project's overall duration.

The SDLC framework is often called *waterfall* because the critical path shown in a Gantt chart often resembles water flowing over a cliff.

After the initial WBS is created, it is adjusted to fit the approved budget and the approved deadline. The resulting project plan shows a detailed list of technical tasks to be performed—all of which are scheduled to produce the project's goal by the approved delivery date.

This plan then is reevaluated and approved by the approval authority, after which work can begin (Gate 1 in the SDLC). Development teams are assembled and assigned to complete tasks as scheduled in the WBS.

What Could Possibly Go Wrong?

It turns out that quite a bit can go wrong. The reason for this is that the SDLC is designed to solve complicated problems. It is *not* designed to deal with complex problems. It works best when the problem to solve is like building that 99th house described in Chapter 2. It is not very well adapted to building the first house.

The waterfall framework assumes that everything relevant to the project is either known at the beginning or can be predicted accurately before any work starts. By the time Gate 1 is passed, an entire plan listing every detail of the work has to have been drawn up. The plan will have to conform to the original budget and delivery date commitments made at Gate 0. The plan is, in effect, a "recipe" for creating the project deliverables. All the developers have to do is follow the recipe and it "should" be possible to achieve all of the project goals.

In reality, creating and following this kind of recipe rarely works. The reason is that the plan is based on the assumption that everything can be predicted before the project starts.

Any typical waterfall plan is filled with dozens (if not hundreds) of assumptions. Every predicted duration of every task in the WBS is an assumption. The completeness and accuracy of the task list itself is an assumption. The belief that the project requirements are correct and will not change is also an assumption. The availability of key developers and other contributors is, once again, an assumption.

There is a wry definition of the word *assume*. "ASSUME: making an ASS out of U and ME." Waterfall plans pile assumptions on top of other assumptions. If any of those assumptions turn out to be unrealistic, the results are often quite bad—if not catastrophic.

The SDLC gating process and associated approvals set a specific expectation in the minds of the approvers. The expectation is that if the detailed plan is approved in Gate 1, then the benefits will be delivered on time and on budget. In effect, the approvers are agreeing to "buy" the results for a fixed price and delivery date. They expect to get those results as long as the project plan they approved is followed.

This expectation is so strong there is usually some kind of "change control" process that restricts the developers' ability to deviate from the approved plan. The assumption is that the plan is correct, so any deviation from it must be incorrect until it is proved otherwise.

The detailed plan and associated Gantt charts give the illusion of certainty about the project's outcome. Success is "guaranteed" if you "plan the work" and "work the plan."

In reality, the detailed plan is usually *wrong*. The duration of each technical task is a *guess*, and the guess is usually made by someone who does not have to do the task him- or herself. They guess at how long a task *should* take. They have no idea how long a task *will* take.

The list of tasks to be performed is also a guess. It is based on the architect's or engineering lead's understanding of the requirement at the beginning of the project before any work has been done. As the work progresses, the need for new tasks may be uncovered. Each new task becomes an item for the change control authority either to approve or disapprove.

The goal of the project is also a guess. At the very beginning of the project, a proposal is reviewed and approved as part of Gate 0. It is approved on the basis of a perceived need that exists at that time. As the project progresses, the need may change. These changes take the form of "requirement change requests," which are also subject to approval by the change control authority.

Waterfall works best for projects that don't involve guesswork. If things such as task lists and durations are known, then the Gate mechanisms and the WBS work well.

In software development, almost all key factors are not known. Using waterfall causes the project plan to boil down to a large number of pure guesses that may be correct or incorrect in the end.

Studies such as the Standish Group 2015 Chaos Report[1] have been made to determine how often waterfall-based software projects are successful. For this purpose, "successful" means the end customer got what they wanted for approximately what they expected to pay and within the approximate timeframe they originally requested.

These studies show that these projects are successful about 11% to 14% of the time. Of the other 86%, about half of those projects are classified as "seriously challenged." "Seriously challenged" means these projects require at least a 50% cost adjustment, 50% rework, and/or a 50% increase in duration to achieve the project's goals. The other half of the 86% represents projects that are total failures, with all costs written off.

In his book *Agile Product Management with Scrum*,[2] Roman Pichler described working through a two-year software development project using the waterfall framework. Throughout the project, a great deal of attention was paid to following the plan. In the end, the project was completed on time and under budget. They planned the work well and worked the plan accurately. Unfortunately, they succeeded in creating a software tool that was perfect for the marketplace as it had existed two years earlier. By the time the project was finished, the end result was obsolete even before it was delivered. The assumption about what the marketplace would need at the end of the two-year project had been wrong. All the time and effort creating the product had been wasted.

Figure 3-1 shows another aspect of the waterfall model that leads to unwanted results. The diagram is based on the work of Deming and others, who maintain that any process that produces a product can be analyzed as a system.

---

[1]Standish Group. *Standish Group 2015 Chaos Report* https://www.projectsmart.co.uk/white-papers/chaos-report.pdf.
[2]Pichler, R. *Agile Product Management with Scrum* (Boston, Ma.: Addison-Wesley Professional, 2010).

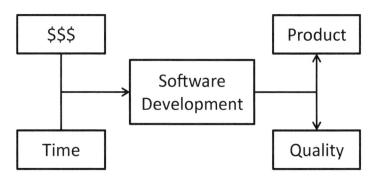

Figure 3-1. Waterfall model

What is a system? A system (such as software development) can be analyzed based on its inputs and its outputs. In other words, the process of software development consumes things and produces things. As Figure 3-1 shows, the software development process consumes money (in the form of people, programming tools, equipment, and so on) and time (man-hours, calendar days). It produces software features and functionality. Most important, however, is that it produces functionality at a certain level of quality.

The important thing to realize is that, in any system, the inputs and outputs are balanced. They form an equilibrium. If the inputs are changed, the outputs change as well.

The WBS in a waterfall project forms a detailed plan to allocate and manage the time and money consumed by the software development process. It dictates that certain functionalities be completed at certain points in time. In effect, the WBS holds constant the inputs (time and resources), but only one of the outputs (functionality).

"Working the plan" means completing all tasks by the dates specified in the WBS using the resources allocated. This works fine if the complexities and durations of all tasks are known. If those complexities and durations are only guesses, however, bad consequences ensue if the guesses turn out to be wrong.

Let's consider an example. Let's assume there is a waterfall project plan for developing a product and that the development team discovers a key task on the plan's critical path has been underestimated. The task had been planned to take two weeks, but the developers now believe it will take five weeks.

Because this task is on the plan's critical path, the delay will affect the entire project. Everything scheduled to be completed after this particular task will be delayed three weeks. The delivery of the product will be delayed three weeks. The budget for the project will be exceeded by three weeks' worth of cost.

Because this change in the schedule has such far-reaching consequences, it usually must be approved by the change control authority before being allowed. The developers must give a justification for taking five weeks instead of two weeks, and they may only take the extra time if the change control authority approves the request.

Often such a change control request is never made. The usual reaction to the news of the potential delay is for the project manager (PM) to tell the developers, "We can't miss this deadline." The PM tells the developers they must stick to the original two-week timeframe. The PM says, "I don't care how you do it. You must get it done in two weeks [or else . . .]."

Faced with this kind of pressure from the PM, the developers often do "figure out" how to get the task done in two weeks. Whether the PM objects or the change control authority rejects the change request, developers are often put in a position in which they are expected to do the impossible. Because the PM doesn't care how they do it, the developers use shortcuts, hard coding, patches, and other bad practices to make it appear they have done the job and met the deadline.

This behavior is clearly predicted by the diagram of the software development system in Figure 3-1. The developers have discovered that the time set aside for a particular task is not adequate. They are told they have to complete the task in the originally specified two weeks. The inputs (resources and time) as well as one of the outputs (product) are all being held constant and fixed. The only way to compensate is to reduce the quality of the product.

The developers do not intend to do a poor-quality job. They simply want to show they have met the deadline so that management will get off of their backs. They do their shortcuts, hard coding, and workarounds while saying to themselves, "We'll come back and fix all of this later." The trouble is, "later" never comes.

Strict adherence to deadlines causes bad code and other quality compromises to corrupt the product. What is worse is that this corruption is hidden. The developers know it's there, but their managers do not.

There is a name for these hidden problems. It is called *technical debt*. Technical debt is work that is "owed" to the product. The truly bad thing about technical debt is not that it exists, but that it is hidden. Technical debt is a problem, but it will never be solved until decision makers realize it is there.

How serious an issue can technical debt become? The following pages present two examples.

The .CSS File from H*LL.

I consulted with a company with a main product that was an e-commerce web site. They had been developing this web site using an aggressive waterfall schedule.

I asked the various PMs and program managers how clean the code base was. They all assured me the quality of the code was "great."

I then asked some of the developers how clean the code base was. They told me it was "awful."

The developers gave me an example of a cascading style sheet (.css) file with which they had to work. (For those of you who are not web designers, a .css file contains rules about the fonts, color schemes, and button shapes used to control the appearance of a web page.)

These .css files are usually not very complicated. A typical .css file contains a few hundred lines of code. A truly complicated one can be 500 to 900 lines long.

The .css file the developers told me about was quite a bit bigger than 500 lines of code. That file had *40,000* lines of code in it! (I could barely stop laughing when I heard how big the file was.)

How did the file get so big? The answer lies in how a .css file works. When a web browser uses it, it reads the file from top to bottom. Whenever it encounters a new rule for displaying a particular part of the web page, it takes note of it. If it encounters a second version of the rule for displaying that particular part of the web page, it forgets the first rule and uses the second one.

When the .css file was relatively new, one of the developers was pressed for time. The job was to change the appearance of a particular part of the web page. Rather than take the time to find the original rule and change it, the developer simply added a new version of the rule to the end of the file.

As more and more changes were required, developers pressed for time simply chose to add new rules to the end of the file, rather than look through the file to find the original version and change it.

At some point in time, the file became too big for anyone to figure out. The only practical way to change a rule was to add a new definition to the end of the file. By the time I talked with the developers, the file contained 12 or more definitions of each and every rule.

The file was so big, it was affecting the performance of the entire web site. It took time for a web browser to read and interpret 40,000 lines of .css code rules. Some developers noted it was possible to log in to a competitor's web application and start completing transactions before their own web site even came up for display.

The real problem with the.css file is not that it was so big. The issue is that the size problem was hidden. It was an "elephant in the living room" that the developers all knew about, but the architects and managers did not. The people who created the Work Breakdown Schedules for various projects assumed the .css file was of normal size. When they planned out the development schedule, they only allocated a small amount of time for changing the appearance of the web site. This forced the developers to take the "easy" way out and perpetuate the problem, rather than fix it once and for all.

A Small Change

Another example comes from another company with which I once consulted. The company's product was also an e-commerce application with a web site, an Android app, and an Apple iPhone (IOS) app as ways for a customer to access it.

Once again, the focus at this company was about aggressive deadlines. The team I worked with once gave an estimate of 90 days to complete a particular enhancement. The top management of the company told the team that 90 days was "ridiculous" and they had only 40 days to complete the work.

One of the consequences of this could be seen in the execution of another enhancement. The team was responsible for enhancing a set of application program interfaces (APIs) that allowed the IOS and Android apps to access the functionality provided by the "core" systems. The Android and IOS people asked for a change in one of the APIs.

The requested change was relatively simple. There was an existing API that the mobile devices called and returned certain pieces of information. The app people simply wanted that API to return three new pieces of information. What's more, those three new pieces of information were already present in the core systems.

The APIs were written in Java and, when asked, most Java programmers would say that this change was probably about an afternoon's worth of work. A Java programmer should be able to sit down and produce this change in a matter of a few hours. Throw in a day or two for testing and the job would be done.

In reality, it took much longer than an afternoon for this enhancement to be made. In the end, it took *four* programmers *six weeks* to get the job done. It took that long because the API code was so bad it was almost impossible to figure out what was going on within it. Also, it was almost impossible to figure out where those three pieces of information were to be found in the core systems.

The whole process became a huge exercise in "trial and error." The developers would return some values only to find out they were the wrong values. They made code changes only to find that the code they changed had been "branched around" and was not even being executed. When they did change some code that was in use, the quality assurance (QA) team reported their change had "broken" something else. It took four developers six weeks to (1) return the correct values and (2) restabilize the API.

How could the management of this company tolerate this kind of situation? The answer is that they didn't notice that it was building up and they didn't realize it was there.

The situation is similar to the story about putting a frog into boiling water. If a frog gets dropped into a pot of hot water, it jumps out immediately. If a frog is put into a pot of cold water that is then gradually heated to the boiling point, it will boil to death before it realizes things are changing.

The management of this company had learned it took a long time to get things done. They kept up constant pressure on the developers, but they also had learned to expect that changes took time. They didn't notice things were getting worse and worse until they got to the point where it took weeks to do what ought to be accomplished in a few hours of work.

Technical debt can be a huge issue. If it is allowed to accumulate, technical debt can become very expensive. It can literally be the difference between the cost of one programmer working for a few hours and the cost of four programmers working for six weeks. Multiply that one example by the number of enhancements a company usually makes to a product and the costs can be staggering.

Technical debt is the result of shortcuts developers take when they can't meet arbitrary deadlines any other way. These deadlines come from guesses that architects and planners make about how long various tasks "should" take. As we have seen, those guesses are usually wrong in the end. Nevertheless, management assumes the overall plan is correct, and all the guesses and assumptions that make it up are also correct. They insist developers "work the plan," even when the plan proves to be unworkable.

Summary

The fundamental root cause of these difficulties is the fact that waterfall is not suitable for doing software development work. Waterfall is designed to solve complicated problems, not complex ones. It is well suited to organizing projects for which there are no uncertainties. If planners and architects really could be certain about the technical challenges and what it will take to solve them, then planning the work and working the plan makes sense.

The challenge is that, in software development, nothing is certain. It is not possible to make a comprehensive plan for developing software because it is impossible to know ahead of time all of the unexpected obstacles that will be encountered along the way,

The only approach that makes sense in software development is an "adaptive" one. First, identify the goal to be achieved (such as a certain piece of software produced for a certain overall cost and delivered within a general period of time). Next, figure out what the first step is and plan that step. Take the step, then look at the results. After taking into account any issues that have been encountered, plan and take the next step. Keep going until either the goal is achieved or it finally makes no sense to continue.

The only way to solve a complex problem is to learn and adapt as you go. The Scrum Framework is an elegant and ingenious way to organize people to do just that.

The Components of Scrum: The Scrum Roles

The Scrum Team

As stated earlier, the Scrum Framework is a way of organizing a product development effort so that it can solve complex adaptive problems.

Products are developed by people. One of the keys to the success of a product is the Scrum Framework's way of organizing people. This also proves to be one of the biggest barriers to the successful adoption of the Scrum Framework by many organizations, large and small.

Scrum organizes people in a structure that is very different from the "traditional" way in which relationships within an organization are defined. Scrum realigns authority, responsibility, and accountability in ways that are very effective, but that fly in the face of conventional wisdom.

Many organizations find these new relationships, authorities, and responsibilities hard to grasp. Traditional structures are based on a "military" model that dates back hundreds of years. The military model, with its different ranks, serves to concentrate decision making (and responsibility) at the top of the organizational pyramid. The higher up an individual is in the structure, the more authority and responsibility that person has. The higher up one is, the more decisions that individual is expected to make.

The Scrum Framework, on the other hand, rejects the hierarchical "military" model. It seeks to align accountability and responsibility with *capability*. Those people who should be held accountable for a certain result are the ones who

© Frederik M. Fowler 2019
F. M. Fowler, *Navigating Hybrid Scrum Environments*,
https://doi.org/10.1007/978-1-4842-4164-6_4

are capable of bringing it about. If they are accountable for a result, they must be given the authority to decide for themselves how to accomplish that result.

Unlike the military model, the Scrum Framework tends to concentrate decision making and responsibility at the *bottom* of the structure. The upper levels of the organization identify goals. The front-line people do the work of achieving those goals and are given authority to *organize themselves* to get it done.

The rest of the Scrum Framework provides tools for people to use when they are organized along Scrum lines. The tools provide ways for people to understand their own progress and to create products effectively. The tools also provide ways for empowered people to work together as a team.

As is often the case, many organizations try to implement the tools in the Scrum Framework without departing from the military model of the organizational structure. When they try to implement Scrum in this way, they are usually bitterly disappointed. The tools of Scrum simply do not work in a "command and control" environment, and trying to make them work usually results in frustration and failure.

The tools of Scrum *only* work when they are used by people empowered to make their own decisions. For people in a "command and control" situation, the tools of Scrum are worse than useless.

Products, Not Projects

The fundamental organizational unit in the Scrum Framework is the Scrum Team. The team consists of a group of people who together create, maintain, and enhance a particular product. The Scrum team takes responsibility for the product and does its work without needing any help from outside the team. The team is initially formed when the product is first created. It remains in existence as long as the product does.

This is quite different from the traditional way of handling products. As indicated earlier, the waterfall model views product development as a series of projects that are undertaken independently. At the beginning of each project, a goal is defined. Budget money is then approved and resources are gathered. A work plan is drawn up and the developers do the technical work required to implement the project goal. At the end of this process, a specific enhancement has been added and the resources are released to be reallocated to other projects.

Scrum departs from the emphasis on "projects." It does so because of its focus on delivering "products of the highest possible value." Organizing work into projects puts the emphasis on achieving project goals. Organizing work around products puts the emphasis on the product and its value.

A Scrum team's job is to engage in an ongoing process of improving the value of the product for which the team members are accountable. Although the individual members of the team can (and do) change over time, the team exists as long as the product exists. They make ongoing changes and improvements to the product until it no longer makes business sense to do so.

The original Scrum Framework was designed for products that could be created and maintained by a group of up to 11 people. This includes the vast majority of software applications other than major commercial ones. In the case of truly huge products, such as the Apache Web Server or Microsoft Word, the Scrum Framework has been extended with the Nexus exoskeleton. A definition and description of Nexus was written by Ken Schwaber in August 2015.[1]

Nexus defines a structure in which three to nine teams can work together to accept responsibility for developing and enhancing a product. The Nexus exoskeleton does not change Scrum's emphasis on the product. It simply expands the resources that can take responsibility for the value of the product.

Cross-functionality

Every Scrum Team must exhibit two vital characteristics. The first of these is *cross-functionality*. For Scrum Teams to play their role effectively, they *must* be cross-functional. If a team is not cross-functional, it cannot function as a Scrum Team.

What does *cross-functionality* mean? It means that a team must have within it every skill set needed to create the product. It does not mean that each team member must possess multiple skills (although that is helpful). Cross-functionality means that each and every skill relevant to creating the product must be present within the Scrum Team's set of developers.

This requirement is often difficult to fulfill when an organization attempts to adopt the Scrum Framework. Traditional teams are usually composed of people with the same skill set. There is a team of programmers, another team of QA people, another one for the database administrators (DBAs), another one for the user experience (UX) people, and so on. In the waterfall model, tasks are assigned to these teams by the PM. It is up to the PM to figure out which team needs to do each task, and to coordinate their work so that each piece fits into the combined result. Coordinating many separate tasks, each in its own "silo," turns out to be quite difficult.

---

[1]*The Nexus Guide*, Scrum.org, 2015 https://www.scrum.org/resources/nexus-guide.

The Scrum Framework, however, strives to eliminate all of those silos. It puts together representatives from those specialties (programmers, QA people, DBAs, UX designers, and so on) into a single team. When the team has been constructed properly, it is able to create the product from start to finish, without any help from anyone outside the team.

Cross-functionality gives two important benefits. The first is that it eliminates delays resulting from dependencies. If, for instance, the programmers have reached a point where they need a DBA, they are dependent on the DBA to do their work before they can proceed. If the DBA is part of the same team as the programmers, the work can be done when the programmers need it. If the DBA is part of an external group, the programmers will have to put in a request and wait for the DBA team to get around to filling their need.

The second important benefit is that it makes it possible for the team to accept responsibility for creating the product. If the team has all the resources it needs to develop and deliver a product, then the team has *no excuses for failing to do so*. If they have to depend on an external DBA, for instance, they can point to the uncertainties about that DBA and that person's priorities as a reason they cannot commit to delivering the necessary functionality. If the DBA is part of the team, the team has no such justification for failing to deliver.

This part of the Scrum Framework makes up part of a "grand bargain" between the organization and the Development Team. The organization gives the Development Team all the skilled resources needed for creating the product. In exchange, the Development Team accepts responsibility for creating the product with no external help.

Self-organization

The second vital characteristic of a Scrum Team is self-organization. To accept responsibility for creating a product, the team *must* be self-organizing. If a team is not self-organized, then it cannot be held accountable for its work product.

With the waterfall framework, there is a Project Manager (PM) who organizes the work of the developers, analyzes the work to be done, assigns various tasks to the various technicians, supervises the work, and deals with any day-to-day adjustments that must be made. The responsibility for making sure the product is created rests with the PM.

In a self-organizing team, there is no PM. *The team manages itself.* The developers analyze the work to be done. The developers divide up the tasks among themselves and monitor their own progress. The developers deal with day-to-day adjustments that must be made. In the end, the responsibility for delivering the product rests with the developers themselves.

One of the flaws in the waterfall framework is the fact that accountability rests solely with the PM. The PM makes all organizational decisions and assigns tasks to the various developers to perform. The developers have no responsibilities other than to do the work that has been assigned to them. The PM accepts almost all the responsibility, and the developers accept almost none of it.

The PM tells the developers, "Do what you are told" In return, each developer tells the PM, "Just tell me what you want me to do and I will do my best."

What are the developers really saying when they tell the PM, "Just tell me what you want me to do"? They are saying they don't have to take any responsibility about whether they are doing the right thing. They will do what the PM asks. If it is the wrong thing, then it is the PM's fault, not theirs.

In addition, when they say, "I will do my best," the developers are really saying, "I will give it a try, but I don't guarantee I will get it done." Once again, it was the PM's decision to give them the task, so if it proves to be too much for them, it is the PM's fault and not their own. And, by saying, "I will do my best," the PM has no way to measure whether the developer is doing their best work. Promising to do their best does not really change anything.

With the waterfall framework, there is a misalignment between accountability and capability. PMs are accountable for everything but have no direct capability to deliver anything. They must rely on the goodwill of the developers to get the project done. The developers generally cooperate until something goes wrong. At that point, the blame game begins, with the developers pointing out they had no say in any of the important decisions.

As I said before, the Scrum Framework serves to align accountability with capability. The developers are the only people who are capable of doing the work needed to create and deliver the product. For this reason, the Scrum Framework requires them to have the authority to organize and manage themselves. There is no PM to take accountability away from them. The developers themselves must assign work, track progress, and make sure they deliver the product as promised.

Self-organization is the second part of that "grand bargain" I mentioned before. Having developers work in cross-functional, self-organizing teams is the only way they can accept responsibility for creating the product. Only if they are (1) given all the skills needed and (2) given permission to organize the work themselves, can they be held responsible for the result. They will have no excuses not to deliver the product if they control the entire development process themselves.

Summary

Scrum Teams *must* be cross-functional and *must* be self-organizing. Only when the developers on the Scrum Team can accept full responsibility for creating a product can they bring all their talents to bear on the problem. We all know that "two heads are better than one." It turns out that three to nine talented people are much better at creating products when they solve problems together, rather than being told what do to.

A properly structured cross-functional team works best when it organizes itself. Managers only get in the way.

Scrum Team Roles

The Product Owner

The Scrum Framework organizes people by defining three distinct sets of responsibilities. Each set of responsibilities is called a *role*, and individuals play different roles when they participate in Scrum teams.

It is important to realize that these roles do not necessarily correspond to actual individuals. It is quite possible for people to play more than one role. It is not uncommon, for instance, for a developer also to play the role of Scrum Master (provided they have the necessary skills and experience to do so). Roles are sets of responsibilities; so, if an individual is capable of fulfilling more than one set, that's fine.

The three roles in the Scrum Framework address the fact that products always have both business and technical dimensions. There is a role—the Product Owner—that takes responsibility for all the business decisions that must be made. There is a second role—the Development Team—that takes responsibility for all of the technical decisions that must be made.

Finally, there is a third role—the Scrum Master—that takes responsibility for making sure the other team members understand and live up to their responsibilities. The Scrum Master makes sure the team uses the Scrum Framework properly.

© Frederik M. Fowler 2019
F. M. Fowler, *Navigating Hybrid Scrum Environments*,
https://doi.org/10.1007/978-1-4842-4164-6_5

The Product Owner

The first role to consider is that of the Product Owner The Scrum Framework's Product Owner role involves guiding the team so the value of the product delivered is the highest possible for the team to produce. In the words of *The Scrum Guide*, the Product Owner's role is to maximize the business value of the product delivered by the team.

The role of Product Owner is *not* a technical role. Although knowledge of a product's underlying technology can be helpful, Product Owners are not responsible for any technical decisions regarding the product.

Product Owners are businesspeople. They must have expertise in understanding the marketplace in which the product will compete. Their job is to make sure the developers are always working on those parts of the product that will be of most value to the organization when they are completed.

In many ways, Product Owners function as investors. Product Owners invest the company's time and money in a team of developers. The goal of Product Owners is to earn a profit on that investment. They earn that return by guiding the developers to deliver valuable additions or changes to the product. The relative success of a Scrum Team Product Owner can be measured by the value of the product in the marketplace.

As stated in Chapter 1, the Scrum Framework focuses on products rather than projects. The reason for this is that the value of products can be measured directly in the marketplace, whereas the value of projects cannot.

Although one Product Owner can own many products, each product must be owned by one and only one Product Owner. That Product Owner must accept accountability for the value of the product.

Product Owner Characteristics

The role of Product Owner involves a considerable amount of responsibility. The individual who plays this role is measured on a "profit and loss" basis and makes decisions about how to spend significant amounts of the organization's resources. This role is usually filled by someone who has the respect and trust of the highest levels of the organization's management team.

Much of the day-to-day work of Product Owners involves negotiation. They negotiate with upper management to get the resources necessary to put together the Scrum Team. They negotiate with customers and stakeholders to identify and prioritize the development of product features. They negotiate with the Development Team to reach agreement about the features and functions that will be developed during each sprint. Product Owners should be people who are skilled at negotiating.

One more crucial characteristic of good Product Owners is their ability to make decisions. Product Owners make choices every day and they have to make them quickly and efficiently. After a decision has been made, it should "stick" and not be revisited lightly.

About ten years ago I was involved in a project to create an e-commerce web site for a distribution company. I was lucky enough to have the perfect Product Owner for the initiative.

The company was very old-fashioned (even for the business climate of 2007). It produced a thick catalog containing all 14,000 or so products it carried. Once a year it would print and mail a copy of this catalog to every one of their 20,000 or so customers. The customers would then leaf through the pages until they found the items they wanted.

After the customers had made a list of their desired items, they would call a toll-free telephone number printed on the cover of the catalog. They would be connected to a customer service person in a call center who would take their order over the phone. The customer service person would then key in the ordered items on an old-fashioned "green screen" terminal and into the mainframe-based order entry system.

This way of taking orders was both expensive and error prone. The costs of printing and mailing the catalog were considerable. There were also accuracy problems caused by taking orders orally ("I asked for ten 20-inch brackets, but you sent me 20 ten-inch brackets."). Something had to be done about the way the company did its business.

That "something" turned out to be the creation of an e-commerce web site. The goal was to create an "electronic catalog" in which customers could search through the company's products and load up a "shopping cart" of the items they wanted. They would then "check out" with their shopping cart, which would feed the orders directly into the mainframe-based order entry system.

As I said, the Product Owner for this "electronic catalog" was the perfect person for the job. He was the chief operating officer (COO) of the organization. As such, he had three very valuable traits:

1. He understood the business at a very fundamental level. He had been with the company for the better part of 30 years and knew just about everything there was to know about it, its products, and its customers.

2. He knew what he wanted. He understood the problems and drawbacks of the existing telephone-based system and he wanted those problems to go away. He also knew what kind of people the customers were and the amount of change they could accept.

3. He could make decisions that no one would question. As the COO, he was the no. 2 ranking person in the entire company and had the authority to shape its operations as he saw fit. If a developer asked him a question about how some particular feature should work, he would give an answer on the spot and that would be that.

Serving on a Scrum Team with a bunch of technical people turned out to be very appealing to the COO. He had a great interest in how technology could help the business, but he also had very naive ideas about what modern technology could and could not do. Working with the developers on the team gave him a way to explore some of his ideas and learn both the capabilities and the limitations of the web site. In the end, he learned to make business decisions while taking technical realities into account.

Having the COO on the team was equally beneficial for the technical people. Their interaction taught the developers about the business and its customers. Among other things, the COO taught the developers that the company's customers were even more old-fashioned than the company itself. Many of the customers were still exploring the use of the "modern wonder" called a *fax machine*. The developers learned the e-commerce web site had to be very simple and needed extensive step-by-step on-screen instructions for how to use it. In the end, the developers learned how to make technical decisions while taking business realities into account.

The fact that the e-commerce web site had the COO as its Product Owner produced wonderful results. Within six months of going live, the web site was doing 30% of the company's business. The number of incorrect shipments and returns dropped, order accuracy improved, and customer satisfaction rose as well. It was a success by any measure.

Common Product Ownership Dysfunctions

Although that COO was the best Product Owner I ever worked with, there have been many I've coached throughout the years who have had trouble filling their role. The dysfunctions I've encountered tend to fall into a few basic categories.

The Product Owner as PM

Quite often Product Owners feel quite a bit of pressure to "deliver" and can then fall into a trap. The trap is to become the de facto manager of the Development Team.

In the Scrum Framework, developers accept accountability for the delivery of the product and then take responsibility for organizing themselves to do so. If they can get someone else to organize them, the developers can then avoid any accountability for what they are doing. They can then say, "Just tell us what you want us to do and we'll do our best." As noted earlier, this statement really boils down to a complete abdication of responsibility on the part of the developers.

I've consulted with clients whose Product Owners have fallen into this trap. One of them had Product Owners who had been "taught" by the developers to write very detailed requirements, including details of both *what* to do and *how* to do it. When I asked one of the Product Owners why his requirements included actual sample code for the developers to use, his answer was, "I have to do it. Whenever the developers do not deliver what I want, the excuse is always 'you didn't put that in the requirements.'"

The most egregious example of a Product Owner acting as a PM involved adding an "e-mail address" column to an existing screen that already contained columns for name and phone number. The developers added a third column, but it was not wide enough to contain a full e-mail address without cutting off the last few characters it contained. Product Owner had asked for the column but had neglected to specify that the column be wide enough to accommodate e-mail addresses.

The developers had done what the Product Owner told them to do, and they had done "their best." The Product Owner let them get away with it by starting to tell them what to do. The Product Owner gave them tasks to do rather than problems to solve. The results were laughable and of little value to anyone.

The Product Owner "Committee"

Another common dysfunction is to have Product Owners who cannot make decisions without consulting others. The easiest way to find out if this is the case is to ask Product Owners to make a decision. If they actually make a decision, then all is well. If their answer to the question is "Let me go check," then that person is a messenger, not a Product Owner.

Product Owners have to negotiate constantly. They negotiate with developers, stakeholders, clients, and third-party partners. Negotiators have to be able to make decisions and stand by them. If negotiators cannot say "yes" to a proposal, then negotiating with them is a waste of time.

One client with whom I've worked in the past had one so called Product Owner for each Scrum team. These individuals were business analysts whose job was to write technical specifications from business requirement documents (BRDs). They had no ability to make any decisions at all.

When asked for clarifications about requirements, all these people could do was to repeat what was documented in the BRDs in the first place. It was futile for developers to suggest different approaches or alternative interpretations. After a while, they gave up.

Another one of my clients had a number of otherwise-capable Product Owners whose decisions were being overridden constantly by upper level management. The C-level people assumed that being "Agile" meant priorities could be changed instantly with no advance notification to anyone. The Product Owners had become frustrated because every time they tried to make strategic decisions about their products, their plans were overturned by some new "corporate initiative." In the end, they stopped making any kind of strategic plan at all. The resigned themselves to bend with every new gust of wind blowing down from the C level. They developed no long-term vision for their products at all.

A Product Owner is one person who is personally accountable for the value of the product. They must provide a single, clear voice, and identify opportunities and priorities for the team to pursue.

The Product Owner Without a Product

Many organizations make the mistake of organizing Scrum Teams around "components" and then assigning each team its own Product Owner. The Product Owner then sets the priorities for the team and controls the growth and development of the component.

The trouble with this approach is that it is very difficult to measure the business value of a component. Surely the component is valuable, but *how valuable*? How can Product Owners measure the relative value of one enhancement over another? How can Product Owners calculate whether they are earning a return for the company on the dollars being invested in the team?

The lack of clarity about what *value* means for a component leads to priority conflicts. For instance, if a Product Owner is asked by a customer to add a new feature to a front-end component, they must negotiate with the Product Owner of the back-end component. The front end cannot produce the necessary API needed to support the new feature by itself. The Product Owner for the front end cannot set priorities for the back end team. The front-end Product Owner has to hope and pray that the back-end Product Owner agrees that the new feature should be produced. Otherwise, nothing will get done.

Conflicts such as these can be solved easily if it is possible to measure the value of the team's work in dollars and cents. It is only possible to do this if there is a way to measure the value of the product itself in dollars and cents.

For example, it is easy to measure the value of a discrete product such as a smartphone-based game. If the game is available from the Google Play Store for $1.99 and 1,000,000 people download it, then the value of the game is $1,990,000. If some enhancement causes another 500,000 people to download it, that enhancement is worth $1.99 × 500,000, or $995,000.

In the component-level example, neither the value of the front end nor the value of the back end can be measured in dollars and cents. Only the *combination* of the front-end and back-end components can produce measureable value in the marketplace.

Rather than having one Product Owner for the front end and one for the back end, it should be recognized that the product is the *combination* of the front end and the back end. Each component can have its own team of developers, but there should only be *one* Product Owner setting priorities and maximizing value.

Product Owner Commitments

Product Owners tend to be busy people, especially if they are placed highly in an organization. They can have multiple demands on their time.

Despite this, and as *The Scrum Guide* makes clear, Product Owners are members of a Scrum Team. They must be a "team player" with the others and must work with them on the basis of mutual respect and trust.

If a highly placed executive consents to play the Product Owner role for a team, that person must commit to be available. The Agile Manifesto makes clear that business people and technical people must work together on a daily basis. Product Owners must be available on a daily basis to interact with the developers, answer their questions, and teach them about the business purpose their work is serving.

One of the reasons that some efforts to adopt the Scrum Framework fail is that new Product Owners misunderstand the demands of the role. If they are placed highly in the company (as, ideally, they should be), their day-to-day activities may change dramatically,

Product ownership is not a role that can be played by writing memos. Interacting with developers is key. As the Agile Manifesto states, the best way to convey information within a team is face-to-face. Product Owners must commit enough time in their schedule to interact directly with their Scrum Team to make sure all business priorities, concerns, and realities are understood by everyone involved.

Summary

As *The Scrum Guide* states, Product Owners' responsibilities are to maximize the value of the work performed by the Scrum Team. They do this by bringing a business perspective to the team to complement the technical abilities of the developers. Commercial software is always created to serve a business purpose. Product Owners take responsibility for articulating that purpose and guiding the team to serve it as best it can.

The Scrum Development Team

The second of the three roles defined by the Scrum Framework is "developer." A Scrum developer is a technical professional who takes part in the creation of the team's product. Developers are typically organized into teams of three to nine people, and together they take responsibility for turning the Product Owner's ideas into working results ready to give to a customer.

When the Scrum Framework was described originally in 1995, the term *developer* was new to the world of software creation. Back then, there were *programmers*, *architects*, *testers*, *technical writers*, and *DBAs*. Scrum introduced the term *developer* as a generic catch-all to refer to any kind of technical professional contributing to the creation of the product.

These days (more than 20 years after the Scrum Framework was introduced), the term *software developer* has taken on a new meaning in common usage. Software developers now do the same kinds of work that "programmers" did in 1995. These days we have *developers*, *architects*, *testers*, and so on. This causes confusion and leads some organizations to believe that Scrum development teams consist of programmers only.

© Frederik M. Fowler 2019
F. M. Fowler, *Navigating Hybrid Scrum Environments*,
https://doi.org/10.1007/978-1-4842-4164-6_6

If you recall from a previous chapter, Scrum development teams must be *cross-functional.* They must have all the different skill sets needed to deliver a finished product. In Scrum, we do not have programmers, architects, testers, and so on. We only have *developers.*

In many organizations today, there are various classifications of people with a particular skill. Someone may be a senior architect or a junior DBA. There may be lead testers and development leads as opposed to ordinary testers and developers. Development Teams may consist of people with a variety of skills, skill levels, and accumulated years of experience.

Although such differences in ability exist, the Scrum Framework recognizes no special distinctions among members of the Development Team. There are no senior developers or junior developers or lead developers. Everyone has the same title: developer.

If everyone on a team has the same title, there is an implied sense that everyone on a team is "equal" in some way. This may seem to fly in the face of common sense, because team members are not equal in their ability to contribute to the overall work product.

However, Scrum Development Team members *are* equal. They are equals in a very important way that is essential to the success of the Scrum Framework.

No two individuals can ever be equal in their capabilities, but the members of a Scrum Development Team are equal in their *responsibilities.* They are all equally responsible for the successful creation of the product.

Much of the interaction between the Development Team and the Product Owner on a Scrum Team involves negotiation. The team and the Product Owner negotiate about the work to be done in a given sprint. When agreement is reached and a scope for a sprint is defined, all the developers must be part of the agreement. Every member must feel and be equally *accountable* for the result.

This shared accountability is one of the keys to the effectiveness of the Scrum Framework. Scrum's roles are designed to make sure that accountability is aligned with *capability.* Only the Development Team has the capability to create the product. For that reason, the Development Team must have control over the creation of the product and be accountable for it.

Just as Scrum recognizes no title other than developer, it recognizes no subteams within the development team. There is no QA subteam or user interface subteam. There is only the Development Team.

The reason for this is that subteams tend to limit the scope of accountability. For example, in a traditional scenario, if a testing effort is "backed up," the DBAs might say, "That's the QA team's problem."

With Scrum, a test backup is *everyone's problem*. It belongs to the entire Development Team, because the entire Development Team told the Product Owner they would deliver something at the end of the sprint that would be "done" and ready to give to the customer.

This sense of collective accountability is very important in the Scrum Framework. Only the developers have the ability to create the product, so they must own the creation of the product. They must make all the decisions that affect the creation of the product and the way they work together.

Self-organization

Self-organization is a concept that is often misunderstood in software development organizations. It is thought, mistakenly, that self-organization is a way for teams to cut bureaucratic red tape and move decision making closer to the "front line." It is true that self-organization often leads to more efficient decision making, but this is not the reason it is a key to the success of the Scrum Framework.

Scrum Development Teams must organize themselves. They collectively must make *every* decision about what to do and how to get the work done; they must make every decision because any decision *not* made by them is a potential excuse for failing to deliver on their promises. Every time a decision is made by someone else, the developers have the opportunity to say, "Thanks for telling us what to do. We will do our best." Every decision made by someone else is owned by someone else, and the consequences are not the developers' problem.

At the beginning of each sprint, the Development Team must choose the work it will do, in agreement with the Product Owner. The team members must also make their own plan to get it done. Only then can they feel that they own the outcome of the sprint,

The Development Team must also make decisions about the tools and infrastructure it will use. Members must negotiate for the necessary server capacity, testing environments, and software development tools they wish to use. Unless they agree with the allocation of these resources to their use, they will have a ready-made excuse for every failure to deliver.

The Development Team must also make decisions about what skills the team needs to have to be cross-functional. In fact, the Development Team must have the final say as to who its team members are. Unless the team chooses its members itself, team members will have excuses to blame each other for each failure.

As problems arise, the Development Team must solve the problems itself. Members must not depend on outside help. Once again, the reason is that any help from the outside can become an excuse for poor performance ("The outsiders said they would fix it and they didn't.").

Let's take a hypothetical example. Let's imagine a development team that has a very skilled JavaScript developer and also a not-so-skilled JavaScript beginner. The skilled one is so skilled she has written books about JavaScript and teaches JavaScript classes for a local university. She has worked with JavaScript since it was invented in the 1990s. There is very little she does not know about the language.

Let's also imagine that the JavaScript beginner has very little experience. He learned JavaScript through an online training course that consisted of "ten easy lessons." He has done the online class exercises but has never written any original JavaScript code professionally. All he has done for the team so far is to make minor changes to existing code.

Let's imagine that the product the development team is creating contains a fair amount of JavaScript code. The next several features on which the team will be asked to work require a good bit of JavaScript coding. The team is not worried because they have an "expert" who can do the JavaScript work quickly and easily.

Finally, let's imagine that one day the expert gets some bad news. Her dear father, who lives 3,000 miles away, has suddenly become very ill and is in the hospital. The expert has to drop everything and rush to his bedside. As she is saying goodbye to her teammates, she lets them know that she will be unavailable for an indefinite period. It could be days, weeks, or even months.

The two questions are: Whose problem is it when the key developer becomes unavailable? Who must figure out what to do?

The answer is: The Development Team must figure it out. The Development Team owns the creation of the product. Therefore, when the unexpected happens, the Development Team must find a solution.

How can the Development Team compensate for the loss of a key resource? Here are some options:

- The inexperienced JavaScript developer can attempt to take on the work, but must be relieved of all other tasks. The Development Team can split up and share the work normally done by the JavaScript beginner to free him up for this challenge.

- If the beginner is not capable of accomplishing the work alone, the Development Team can check with other teams to see if some other team has a JavaScript expert they can "borrow" for a few sprints. They can also arrange a temporary "trade" of their beginner for the other team's expert if the other team's JavaScript needs are less challenging.

- If there is no other expert available, the Development Team can arrange for the hiring of a temporary substitute. The team would ask the Product Owner for budget money to hire a contractor and then work with the human resources department to get some candidates to interview. The team would review the candidates and make a hiring decision as a team.

In all cases just described, the entire team owns the problem of dealing with the missing JavaScript expert. Regardless of the final solution, it must be a solution owned by the entire Development Team. If it is not, and the Product Owner makes the decision, the Product Owner is solely responsible for the consequences of the decision.

For example, imagine what would happen if the Product Owner of the JavaScript-heavy product told the team, "Don't worry. I have the perfect solution. I'll hire my brother-in-law to replace the expert. He can do the job. Trust me!" The brother-in-law becomes an instant excuse for failure: "Of course we failed to deliver. We lost our expert and the Product Owner gave us his stupid brother-in-law instead. What did you expect?"

If the Development Team is to own the delivery of the product, it must have no excuses for failing to deliver. To have no excuses, the Development Team must make *all decisions about how to get the work done*. This includes all "management" decisions, including the hiring and firing of its membership, acquiring third-party resources, and securing an adequate infrastructure for doing its work.

To be a true Scrum Development Team, it must be able to solve its own problems, manage itself, and accept accountability for delivering its product.

Team Size

The members of a Scrum Development Team need to work together well. Ideally, they operate on the basis of mutual respect and trust, and are able to make decisions together quickly. When individuals on the team encounter difficulties, the others must pitch in and help. The team must succeed or fail as a whole.

When these facts are taken into consideration, it should be no surprise that team size is an important factor. If a team is too big, it may not be able to think and act as a whole.

The Scrum Guide gives a recommendation for Development Team size. It recommends that a Development Team be no smaller than three developers and no larger than nine developers. One developer is not a team; two can coordinate their activities without the need for a framework like Scrum. More than nine people can rarely agree on when to go to lunch together, let alone how to deal with a serious challenge. The "three to nine developers" rule is based on years of practical experience on the part of Ken Schwaber and Jeff Sutherland and is a good rule of thumb.

In fact, Jeff Sutherland has made several statements in YouTube videos and at conferences in 2016 and 2017 that the ideal development team size is 4.7 people. He is quoting a recent study by the Harvard Business School as the source of this statistic.

It is important to realize, however, that the "three to nine developers" rule is a recommendation, not a requirement. The real test is whether the team can solve its own problems, manage itself, and accept accountability for creating the product.

Sometimes a team of eight or nine people can be too big. If the eight or nine people can't solve their problems, manage themselves, and accept accountability for creating the product, perhaps the thing to do is reduce the team's size.

Sometimes a team of more than nine people is not too big. I had a conversation once with a Product Owner who was distressed about the size of his team. He said, "Fred, I know my team is too big, but I hate the idea of breaking them up. They work very well together, but according to *The Scrum Guide*, the team is too big."

I asked, "Do they manage themselves?"

He answered, "Yes."

I asked, "Do they solve their own problems?"

Again, he answered, "Yes."

Finally, I asked, "Do they accept accountability for delivering the product?"

He said, "Yes!"

I said, "It seems to me the team is working well and shouldn't be split up. There's nothing broken about the team. Don't try to fix anything."

"Great!" he said happily.

I then asked him, "How many people are there on the team?"

"Twenty four," he replied.

All I could think to myself was that they must be a remarkable set of 24 people if they could indeed be self-organizing. Nevertheless, such things are possible.

Colocation vs. Geographic Distribution

The issue of colocation vs. geographic distribution of team members is a contentious one. For various reasons, some organizations create teams with members who are scattered all over the world. One of my clients has a single team whose members were in India, Europe, Central America, and California.

Is this distribution correct or incorrect? The answer lies in the basic test of whether the team is capable of self-organization. The questions to ask are

- Does the team manage itself?
- Can the team solve its problems?
- Does the team accept accountability for creating the product?

It takes a remarkable set of technicians to be able to self-organize over many different time zones. It isn't impossible, but I believe it is very rare. Also, I doubt that the developers on the distributed team I just described had any say in who they were working with. Needless to say, the amount of value they delivered each sprint was quite a bit less than other teams colocated within the company.

Cross-functionality and self-organization are the keys to aligning the accountability for creating a product with the capability of doing so. The technical people in an organization must be given authority to develop the product as they see fit. Only then can they be asked to accept responsibility for the quality and value of the outcome of their efforts.

Summary

At its heart, the Scrum Framework provides a very simple organizational model. The idea is to pair up someone who knows the business needs to be served (i.e., the Product Owner) with a team of people capable of creating the product the Product Owner needs to have created. The best results happen when the team members of technical professionals have all the tools and skills they need, and are given the freedom to decide how best to do their work by themselves.

The Scrum Master

The third role defined by the Scrum Framework is perhaps the most misunderstood one of all. The Scrum Master role is neither a "business" role nor a "technical" role. The day-to-day work of a Scrum Master is hard to describe in terms of specific tasks to be done. When asked what a Scrum Master does on a day-to-day basis, the proper answer is: It depends. At best, the detailed work of a Scrum Master is vaguely defined and hard to pin down. This causes some organizations to attempt to use the Scrum Framework without the benefit of qualified Scrum Masters, usually with less-than-desirable results.

Once again, the role of Scrum Master on a Scrum Team is defined in terms of *responsibilities* as opposed to tasks. The Scrum Master has significant responsibilities that no one else bears. Addressing those responsibilities can take many shapes and forms. The Scrum Master adds value by accepting and acting on those responsibilities. The value is usually easy to see and measure when comparing the results of a team with an effective Scrum Master with those of a team with no Scrum Master.

The word *master* in the name Scrum Master implies a kind of authority. Some people think a Scrum Master is some kind of task master, someone with a whip who drives slaves to work hard.

In fact, a Scrum Master is the master of *no one*. A Scrum Master is a *master of the Scrum Framework.* A Scrum Master is a master of Scrum in the same way that a Kung Fu master is a master of the art of Kung Fu.

© Frederik M. Fowler 2019
F. M. Fowler, *Navigating Hybrid Scrum Environments*,
https://doi.org/10.1007/978-1-4842-4164-6_7

Like a Kung Fu master, the role of a Scrum Master is to be a teacher, mentor, and coach. The Scrum Master teaches and coaches the Product Owner and Development Team how to use the Scrum Framework properly. More specifically, the Scrum Master's responsibility is to make sure the Product Owner and the Development Team understand and live up to *their* responsibilities.

To function properly, a Scrum Team must have a Product Owner who focuses on maximizing value and a Development Team that focuses on technical execution. Both must work together on the basis of mutual respect and trust. In short, the Scrum Team must truly function as a high-performance team.

The Scrum Master is responsible for the Scrum Team's ability to function as a team. The Scrum Master owns the team's "teamwork." Just as a coach in the world of sports teaches players how to play together effectively, a Scrum Master teaches developers and Product Owners how to work together effectively.

Product Owners tend to be people in positions of power within a company, and they make decisions involving large amounts of the company's resources. They accept considerable responsibility and are held accountable for results. For this reason, there is a natural tendency for these people to become "bosses" and to give orders about what is to be done.

Developers tend to be individual contributors who feel they have little or no power within an organization. They tend to play a passive role and often resort to passive-aggressive tactics when confronted with unpleasant situations. For these reasons, there is a natural tendency for these people to become "peons" and to ask to be told what to do.

The Scrum Master's main work is to teach and coach everyone to combat these natural tendencies. The Scrum Master teaches the developers to take an active role, set expectations, and live up to them. The Scrum Master teaches the Product Owner to set priorities, negotiate with the developers to get them addressed, and then trust the developers to live up to their end of the negotiated bargain.

When qualified and able people play their proper roles on a Scrum Team, the results can be spectacular. Unfortunately, there are often organizational, cultural, and personality-based pressures that prevent people from playing these roles correctly.

The Scrum Master's job is to teach and coach the team to resist these pressures. The specific challenges faced by the Scrum Master change every day. The goal, however, remains the same: to take a group of professional individuals and help them to form an identity in which the whole is greater than the sum of its parts.

Teaching People to Solve Their Own Problems

The roles on a Scrum Team can be compared to the roles on a professional sports team, such as an NBA basketball or NHL hockey team. On such a team, the players are seen as similar to the developers, and the team owner is recognized as playing the Product Owner role. The analog for the Scrum Master is the head coach on the sidelines.

Head coaches do not play the game, nor do they make financial decisions. The know their players know how to play their various positions (otherwise, they would not be on the team at all.) They know the team owner will keep the finances in order. The head coach job is to (gently) keep the owner from interfering with the players, and to get the players to work together effectively. Needless to say, it is a full-time job, and no professional sports team operates without a coach.

The Scrum Master's job is quite similar to that of a sports coach, but in this case, to keep the Product Owner from interfering with the developers, and to get the developers to work together effectively. It is also a full-time job, and no professional Scrum Team should operate without a Scrum Master.

Just as a professional basketball coach watches the action from the sidelines, a Scrum Master watches the team without becoming part of the work being done. The Scrum Master's job is to get everyone else to do the work necessary to create the product. Another way of putting it is: The Scrum Master's job is to make sure team members do not have an excuse for not fulfilling their responsibility.

Scrum Masters must make sure the Development Team owns every part of delivering the product features prioritized by the Product Owner. Scrum Masters must also make sure the Product Owner owns every part of the product's content and value. Scrum Masters can give advice and help out with details if asked, but in the end they must make sure all technical decisions are made by the Development Team and all business decisions are made by the Product Owner.

Servant Leadership

The Scrum Guide states that a Scrum Master is a "servant leader" for the team. Servant leadership is a slippery concept that confuses many people. After all, how can a servant lead the way?

The best way that I have found to describe servant leadership is to point to a historical example of a very effective servant leader. If the role played by this man is considered and understood, the concept of servant leadership becomes clear.

This man's name was Tenzing Norgay. He was a Sherpa and lived in the Himalayan Mountains of Nepal. In 1953, a British mountain climber named Edmund Hillary arrived in Norgay's village and hired him to lead the way up the slopes of Mount Everest—the tallest mountain in the world.

Hillary and Norgay set out in late spring and made their way up the mountain. Norgay led Hillary up the mountain paths to the ice fields, helped Hillary climb up through the ice and snow, helped him cross crevasses, kept him from falling off several cliffs, and got him to the lower edge of the north face of the mountain. He then helped Hillary climb up the final rocky slopes, cope with the fierce winds, and approach the summit. And, by the way, Norgay carried most of the luggage as well.

No one alive knows what happened when Hillary and Norgay reached the very top of the summit, but rumor has it that Norgay stepped up to the top and then extended a helping hand to Edmund Hillary, who thus became *the first man ever to climb Mount Everest!*

Norgay then did something for Hillary that is arguably more important than getting him to the top of Everest. Norgay got Hillary back down again. He got Hillary back down the north face, back down through the ice fields, back over the crevasses, back down the mountain paths, and finally back to the village where they had started.

This was very significant because, many years earlier, a pair of very experienced climbers had attempted to climb the mountain. They were George Mallory and Andrew Irvine, and they may well have reached the top. No one knows, however, because they never came down again. Mallory's remains were discovered on the mountain by American climber Conrad Anker in 1999.

After Hillary and Norgay reached the village, they said their farewells. Hillary went back to fame and fortune in Europe and America, and Norgay went back to village life. Eventually he made a kind of business out of guiding people up the mountain. He died in May 1986 at the age of 71.

A servant leader's job is similar to that of Tenzing Norgay. The servant leader helps others achieve their goals, keeps them from "falling off the cliffs," keeps them safe, but enables them to do great things. Servant leaders do not take credit for success. Their reward is to enable the success of others.

Scrum Masters would do well to remember the example of Tenzing Norgay and focus on enabling their teams to be successful within the Scrum Framework.

Impediments

The Scrum Guide does list one specific duty the Scrum master must perform. The Scrum master must remove impediments to the development team's progress. This "impediments" requirement is easily misunderstood and often gets new Scrum Masters in trouble. It is very important to understand *what constitutes an impediment.* Many "blockers" that inexperienced Scrum Masters spend time and effort solving are not impediments at all.

Scrum Masters are teachers and coaches. As such, their job is to *teach and coach people to solve their own problems.* Any problem Scrum Masters solve for the team becomes their responsibility to solve whenever it occurs in the future. If they cannot solve it, the developers have a perfect excuse not to deliver the results they agreed to deliver. "We couldn't get it done because the Scrum Master didn't solve our problem."

The Scrum Master must teach and coach the team to solve its *own* problems whenever and wherever possible. Having said that, there are instances when teaching and coaching the team to solve a problem is *not* possible. There are some problems that are too difficult for the team to solve by itself. That is where the Scrum Master must step in.

An impediment is a problem that team members cannot be expected to solve by themselves. Only if it is beyond the capability of the team to resolve should Scrum Masters take ownership and solve it.

Inexperienced Scrum Masters allow teams to saddle them with piles of miscellaneous work in the name of removing impediments. Team members say, "Scrum Master, I can't move forward until I talk with the lawyers. Please arrange a meeting with them for me." They may also say, "Please book a room for us to talk over a design issue" or "Please look into getting us an upgraded version of our software tools." They may go so far as to say, "Please get me a faster workstation" or even "Please get the lights over my desk fixed."

Scrum Masters must exercise judgment with regard to whether a problem can be solved by the team. The team's ability to deal with problems changes over time. If a team is new and its members don't know much about how to request software upgrades, Scrum Masters may choose to do it for them, but *show them how to do it.* Later, when asked to get further upgrades, Scrum Masters might say, "Why should I do that? I showed you how to do it months ago. Please do it yourself!"

Scrum Masters must push back any problems to the team that, in the Scrum master's opinion, can be addressed by the team or its members. The team should arrange its own meetings, book its own rooms, get its own software upgrades, get its own workstations upgraded, and get its own lights fixed. The team must own all aspects of delivering the product, and this includes all of the miscellaneous tasks that make the delivery possible.

Having said that, there is never a time when true impediments cannot occur. Sometimes Scrum Masters must step in when it is clear the team cannot solve a problem itself. These issues tend to be the nastiest, dirtiest, most unpleasant situations that, unfortunately, can and do occur.

During my career I've had developers come to me and say, "I don't know what to do. I saw Suzy going through Brenda's purse." I've also had people say, "Mark is taking drugs all the time." The issue that always causes the most action is when someone—for example, Carol—says something like, "Pete won't keep his hands off me. I've told him to leave me alone but he keeps following me around."

Some issues go beyond the team's boundaries and raise concerns that the human resources department or even local authorities must deal with. In these situations, Scrum Masters must step up and intervene. They must do whatever is necessary to protect the company and the team, and to help keep the team's focus on delivering the product.

Summary

The role of Scrum Master is crucial for a team to reap the benefits of the Scrum Framework. The effectiveness of Scrum Masters is reflected in the quality of the teams they coach, and can be measured objectively.

If Product Owners are ineffective, that ineffectiveness can be measured by the lack of value produced by the team. If the team works hard, creates features, and delivers working software regularly, there is an ineffective Product Owner if the software turns out to have little value.

If Development Teams are ineffective, that ineffectiveness can be measured by the lack of working software produced. If they work hard but can't seem to get anything done, it may be time to reassess team members and create a more effective Development Team.

If Scrum Masters are ineffective, that ineffectiveness can be measured by a team's inability to work together. If the developers are always squabbling among themselves and the Product owner resorts to barking orders at them, it may be time to get a more effective Scrum Master to fix the situation.

A good Scrum Master's contribution is often hard to see, because when Scrum Masters are effective, everything works as it is supposed to. It is only when Scrum Masters are ineffective or absent that their real value becomes apparent.

The Components of Scrum: The Scrum Artifacts

Scrum Artifacts

There are three main components of the Scrum Framework:

1. Scrum roles
2. Scrum artifacts
3. Scrum events

As we have seen, the Scrum roles describe people and their relationships on a Scrum Team. These roles define an organizational structure that is well suited to engage in a process of discovery.

Scrum artifacts and Scrum events are tools that are used by Scrum Teams. These tools allow the Scrum Teams to implement the theory of Empirical Process Control. This theory holds that all decisions must be made on the basis of measurements of reality, rather than predictions of future outcomes.

The three main principles of Empirical Process Control are as follows:

1. **Transparency:** Everything that is or can be known about a subject or object of scrutiny must be available and accessible to everyone involved in any way. Nothing may be hidden; everything must be out on the open and "on the table."

2. **Inspection:** If transparency exists, those people who are involved must inspect that transparency on a regular, formal basis.

© Frederik M. Fowler 2019
F. M. Fowler, *Navigating Hybrid Scrum Environments*,
https://doi.org/10.1007/978-1-4842-4164-6_8

3. **Adaption:** If transparency is inspected on a regular, formal basis, then lessons from that inspection should be learned. Future decisions should be based on lessons learned from past activities.

There are three Scrum artifacts defined in *The Scrum Guide*:

1. The Product Backlog
2. The Sprint Backlog
3. The Sprint Increment

These Scrum artifacts are all designed to implement, aid, and serve the need for transparency. Each artifact makes something clear.

These artifacts are used in Scrum events. Each Scrum event is an opportunity to put Empirical Process Control to use. Each event is an opportunity for the team to inspect the transparency provided by one of the artifacts and to adapt something as a result.

The Sprint Increment

The most basic Scrum artifact is the Sprint Increment. The Sprint Increment is nothing more than the work product of the Development Team during the Sprint event.

The Sprint Increment is defined as the difference between the product at the end of a sprint when all necessary work has been completed, and the product at the beginning of that sprint before any sprint work has been done. It is called an *increment* because it represents what has been "added" throughout the course of the sprint. *The Scrum Guide* defines a product as the cumulative sum of all of the Sprint Increments since the product was first introduced.

The Sprint Increment is an artifact because it is inspected and makes something clear as a result. What does the Sprint Increment make clear? It provides transparency about the current working features and functionality of the product at the end of each sprint. Those features and functions are inspected at the end of every sprint, and future plans are adapted accordingly.

Each Scrum event is an opportunity to inspect and adapt something. The Sprint Increment is inspected during a Scrum event called the *Sprint Review*. During these reviews, the current state of any product is inspected by Product Owners and any guests they may invite. A conversation ensues about what the product does now (as seen by inspecting the increment) and what it could do in the future. Ideas about future functionality are noted by the Product Owners and are added to the Product Backlog if appropriate. Thus, during sprint reviews, Sprint Increments are inspected and Product Backlogs are adapted.

Summary

Scrum Development Teams are groups of technical people who manage themselves to create finished products. The tools of Empirical Process Control are what they use to do so. A key requirement of Empirical Process Control is transparency. The purpose of the Scrum artifacts is to provide the transparency needed for Scrum Team members to understand what they are doing.

The purpose of the Sprint Increment is to make clear the true state of the product as it is being developed. It is examined at the end of every sprint to generate ideas about what further changes and enhancements might be made in the future.

The Product Backlog

One of the most important artifacts in the Scrum Framework is the Product Backlog. Like the other artifacts, its purpose is to make something transparent and clear. It is managed and maintained by the Product Owner, and its purpose is to make clear the plan for developing a product and the sequence in which the product's features and functions are to be created.

The Definitive "Wish List" for a Product

Every product that exists has some kind of list of future enhancements that may or may not be made to it, depending on present and future business conditions. Sometimes this document is referred to as a *product road map*. Sometimes it is called a *comprehensive release plan*. In the Scrum Framework, it is referred to as a *Product Backlog*.

Unlike traditional road maps and release plans, the Product Backlog contains only descriptions of enhancements and an indication of their priority for development. It does not attempt to *schedule* the delivery of these features and enhancements in any way.

There are no due dates attached to Product Backlog items (PBIs). There are only business priorities. The assumption is that higher priority items will be completed and delivered before lower priority items are addressed. The schedule for delivery of PBIs is not set, but the anticipated *sequence* of delivery is.

© Frederik M. Fowler 2019
F. M. Fowler, *Navigating Hybrid Scrum Environments*,
https://doi.org/10.1007/978-1-4842-4164-6_9

Product Backlogs exist as long as their products do. The first step to take when creating a new product is to create its Product Backlog. This is done by writing down a list of the features the new product will have. After the first version of the product is developed and released, new additions and enhancements may be gathered in the Product Backlog to be created for future versions. Work continues in this way until the product reaches the end of its life. The Product Backlog is finally closed out when enhancing the product no longer makes any sense from a business point of view.

It goes without saying that any product should have only one set of priorities for its development. If there are several lists of priorities managed by different people, the result is chaos. A product may have only one Product Backlog, and a Product Backlog may contain only the priorities for the development of a single product.

Likewise, any product should have one and only one person who is accountable for its business success. That person is the one who should make decisions about the features the product should have and choose which features are the most important to develop first.

The Scrum Framework vests responsibility for the Product Backlog with the Product Owner. Product Owners are the ones who may add, change, or delete items in the Product Backlog. The Product Owner is the only person who may set priorities for the items in the Product Backlog.

When a Development Team does its work, it always works from the Product Backlog of a particular product. Each Development Team must work from only one set of priorities, so it may work on only one product and with one product owner at a time.

In addition, if Product Owners are to be accountable for the value the Development Team delivers, they must control the scope of work the Development Team undertakes. For this reason, developers are only allowed to work on items that appear in the Product Backlog and must respect the priorities set by the Product Owner.

A Product Backlog is a repository for all the additions, changes, and enhancements that are planned to be made for a product over time. It contains descriptions of each change and it is owned and maintained by the Product Owner. The items in the Product Backlog are sequenced by the Product Owner according to their importance in delivering value. At any given time, the Product Backlog contains the entire development plan for a product as it is known at that time.

The Product Backlog is the source of the Product Owner's authority. A Product Owner is accountable for the business value produced and delivered by the Scrum Team, so the Product Owner must control the list of changes and enhancements the team may produce. In the Scrum Framework, the

Development Team may work only on items that appear in the Product Backlog. The Product Backlog may only be added to or changed by the Product Owner. Thus the Product Owner controls the changes that may be made to a product and can be held accountable for choices made about them.

Each PBI is a description of some content, feature, or function of the product as seen from the consumer's point of view. Each item must be a partial answer to the question: What should the product do? It should describe some feature, function, or characteristic that will add to the value of the product when completed. It should also describe something that can be demonstrated as complete and working when work on the item has been finished.

The items in a Product Backlog should represent problems to be solved as opposed to tasks to be performed. For example, a useful PBI might be "There needs to be a way for users to log in" as opposed to "Create a user login screen." Creating a screen limits the developers' options for filling the need. Solving the problem of providing a way to log in allows developers to explore many technical options, such at third-party login (e.g., log in with Google) or even biometric identification (using the fingerprint reader available on most smartphones). The Product Backlog should strive to be very clear on the need to be filled, and lets the developers come up with their own strategies for filling the needs.

A product may have one and only one Product Backlog. There must be one and only one plan for the development of the product, one set of goals, and one set of priorities. If there are multiple plans with conflicting priorities, the result is chaos.

A product may have one and only one Product Owner. If more than one person is accountable for the value of a product, then no one is accountable for the value of that product.

The "User Story" Form

PBIs are often written using a particular format. This format is called the *user story form* and it takes the shape of a sentence that tells us who is involved, what they want to do, and why they care about this item. The general form is as follows:

> *"As a [person] I want to [action] so that [reason].",*

where [person] is someone who is involved, [action] is some feature of the product, and [reason] speaks to the need the person sees and knows needs filling.

For example, in the user story

> As an **administrator**, I wish to **reset passwords** so that the **customers can log in easily without becoming frustrated**,

the person is an administrator. Among other things, it can be assumed that the function is for someone who has knowledge about and experience working with the product.

The action is to reset passwords.

The reason is to prevent frustration on the part of customers. They want to be identified to the system and to have access to their private information. They do not want to fight through a difficult and complicated identification and verification process.

Acceptance Criteria

The user story form is very useful for describing the *general* problem to be solved. Most often, though, the user story must be supplemented by adding specifics needs to it. These needs take the form of *acceptance criteria*. These criteria specify specific tests that must be passed before the implementation of the user story solution is deemed "acceptable."

User stories themselves tend to describe the behavior of the product when all goes well. The story "As an account holder, I want to change my login credentials from time to time so that they become harder to guess by an intruder" describes a positive need that can be fulfilled in a number of ways. It describes the so-called *happy path scenario*.

Most often, this happy path scenario needs to be qualified with instructions about what to do when all does not go well. What should be done, for instance, when users try to change their credentials to "blank?" What if they change their credentials to a value they used previously? What if they change their password to "password?"

Acceptance criteria provide a way to qualify a user story so that the "happy path" is accompanied by an appropriate number of *negative scenarios* that describe its function further.

For instance, the following acceptance criteria might be used to qualify the "change login credentials" user story:

- If I try to change the credentials to "blank," I should see an error message that says "blank" credentials are not allowed. I should be asked to try again.

- If I try to change the credentials to a word in the Oxford English Dictionary, I should see an error message that says dictionary words are too easy to guess and are not allowed. I should be asked to try again.

- If I try to change the credentials back to a value I used within the past four changes, I should see an error message that says recent passwords are not allowed. I should be asked to try again.

When specified well, these acceptance criteria serve two valuable purposes. First, they guide the developers on the team to create functionality that takes these "negative scenarios" into account. Second, they form the basis of the acceptance tests needed to validate the proper working of the new functions. This combination of effects has led to a codification of the practice. It is called *acceptance test-driven development*, or ATDD for short. It is one of the families of practices that are collectively known as *Extreme programming*.

Other Forms: Behavior-Driven Development

The user story form is not the only template for describing functionality in the product backlog. Another syntax that is gaining popularity is known as the *behavior-driven development (BDD) form*. This form attempts to describe the behavior desired and the contexts in which that behavior is required.

The BDD form is based on a series of statements using the keywords *given*, *when*, and *then*:

- *Given* that users wish to change their password

- *Given* that users have used the password "123xyz@@" as one of their prior four passwords

- *When* the users attempt to change their password to "123xyz@@"

- *Then* a message should be shown that says duplicated passwords are not allowed

- *Then* users should be given another chance to change the password

In this form, the *given* statements set the contexts, the *when* statements specify the action, and the *then* statements describe the results.

The BDD form not only describes functionality in a way that is straightforward for developers to implement, but also it lends itself to the automation of the acceptance testing effort. BDD is often used in conjunction with a tool called *Cucumber*. Cucumber reads BDD form requirements (called *gherkins*) and translates them into "unit test" calls using tools such as J-Unit. The result is a combination of high-level requirements written in a language understandable to nontechnical people, and low-level testing that is conducted directly from these requirements. The approach is gaining popularity.

The Product Backlog as a Forecasting Tool

Traditional product road maps are often used to define schedules and deadlines. The theory of Empirical Process Control maintains that predictions of future events are inherently inaccurate and can lead to bad outcomes. For that reason, the Product Backlog contains no deadlines. It does not define any kind of fixed schedule for the development of the product.

Although Empirical Process Control states it is impossible to predict what *will* happen by a given point in time, it is possible to get an idea of what is *likely* to happen by a given point in time. The Product Backlog can be combined with measurements of actual activity to provide *forecasts* for the development of the product.

Let's assume there is a Product Backlog containing 100 items of equal size. Let's also assume that a Development Team has been working on the backlog and has been able to complete roughly five items per sprint. It is impossible to say exactly when the 100th item will be completed by the team, but based on what we know now and based on the measured capacity of the team, we can forecast that the 100th item will be completed 20 sprints from now.

It is important to stress the inherent uncertainty about future events whenever one is asked to make predictions about them. Making predictions is risky because predictions often imply a degree of precision and certainty where none is warranted.

There are two important qualifiers that should always be used: *based on what we know now* and *based on the measured capacity of the team.*

What do we know now? We know what the unfinished items on the Product Backlog are. We can make a forecast based on what they are at the moment, but the fact is that the Product Backlog can change at any time. The Product Backlog on Tuesday may look quite different from the Product Backlog on Monday. The content of the Product Backlog depends on the ongoing process of discovery that the Scrum Framework facilitates. Any forecast is uncertain because the content of the Product Backlog itself is uncertain.

What is the "measured capacity of the team?" It is the average amount of work the team accomplishes each sprint, measured according to the size of the PBIs it completes. If a team has completed an average of five PBIs per sprint in the past, its capacity is described as "five PBIs per sprint." This capacity (also known as *velocity*) tends to remain fairly constant as long as the makeup of the team does not change.

Teams do change, though. People leave to get their dream jobs elsewhere. New people join with the hope of obtaining more and better experience. The measured velocity of a team last month may have no relevance to the team that exists now.

The Product Backlog does not provide the imagined certainty of a fixed schedule. It does, however, provide a realistic forecast of what is likely to happen and when it is likely to take place. These forecasts can be used to plan actions that are dependent on the accomplishment of certain milestones. It is not possible to know exactly when milestones will be achieved ahead of time. Using the information provided by the Product Backlog and the team's velocity measurements, it is possible to make a pretty good guess.

The Product Backlog as a Status Reporting Tool

The Product Backlog's purpose is to provide *transparency*. It is often referred to as an *information radiator* that provides important facts to whoever examines it.

Most traditional status reports are also meant to provide transparency. They are requested (or required) whenever management wants to know

- What is being worked on now?
- When will the current work be finished?
- What is next?
- When will that be finished?
- And so on.

The Product Backlog provides all this information—to the extent that this information can be known at any given point in time.

Does the Product Backlog tell us what is being worked on now? The answer is yes. The PBIs that have been accepted into the current sprint are what is being worked on now.

Do we know when the current set of PBIs is to be completed? The answer is yes. They are to be completed by the end of the current sprint.

Do we know what is next? The answer is probably. Using the Product Backlog and the team's velocity, we can make a forecast as to which items will be "next."

Do we know when the next items will be complete? The answer is yes. Whatever the next items are, they should be complete by the end of the next sprint.

And so on.

Summary

In summary, the Product Backlog is a Scrum artifact with the purpose of making several things transparent:

- A complete list of all the product's features and functions as the Product Owner understands them as of that moment

- A ranking of the importance of those features and functions, which serves as a rough sequence for when they will be implemented

- A forecast timeline for the development of the product based on the current contents of the Product Backlog and the current measured capacity of the Development Team to implement the items in the Product Backlog

- Information about what is being worked on at the moment and when it is expected to be completed

The Product Backlog is a single artifact that replaces many other traditional ones used in other frameworks. It is simple, elegant, and effective.

The Sprint Backlog

The third artifact used in the Scrum Framework is the Sprint Backlog. Once again, the purpose of this artifact (and of the other two) is to provide transparency that can be inspected. To understand how this artifact is used, it is necessary to understand how and why it is created.

The Product Backlog exists as long as the product does. Likewise, the Sprint Backlog exists as long as its sprint lasts. It is created at the beginning of each sprint and is discarded as soon as its sprint is over.

The Sprint Backlog is created during the *Sprint Planning Meeting*, an event that starts each sprint. The Sprint Planning Meeting is an event during which the Product Owner and the developers meet, negotiate, and agree on the scope of the work to be done during the sprint. The Product Owner and the Development Team agree on a *sprint goal*, which is an overall statement about the fundamental purpose of the sprint. After the sprint goal is set, the Product Owner and the Development Team negotiate and agree on a set of PBIs on which to work that will satisfy the sprint goal.

When the negotiation is over and the agreement has been reached, the Product Owner leaves. The second part of the Sprint Planning Meeting then starts. The purpose of this second part of the meeting is for the Development Team to make a plan for implementing the agreed-on PBIs. The selected PBIs and the plan for implementing them together make up the Sprint Backlog.

© Frederik M. Fowler 2019
F. M. Fowler, *Navigating Hybrid Scrum Environments*,
https://doi.org/10.1007/978-1-4842-4164-6_10

It is important to recognize that PBIs and Sprint Backlog items are fundamentally different things. When written correctly, Product Backlog items identify *business problems* that are to be solved. Sprint Backlog items, however, identify *technical tasks to be performed*. PBIs answer the question: What problem is to be solved? Sprint Backlog items answer the question: How are we going to solve it?

For example, let's suppose there is a PBI that states, "As a user, I want to log on to the web site so that I can access my private information." If the Development Team accepts this PBI into its sprint, the members must break down this business problem into a number of technical tasks they will perform. A sample list of these technical tasks might consist of the following:

- Write the HTML needed to show user ID and password boxes on the page, plus a Submit button labeled "Log On."

- Write the JavaScript needed to capture the button press and make an API call to the back-end system for validation.

- Write the code on the back-end system to implement the API and validate the supplied username and password against the user database.

- Create the appropriate tables needed for the user database. And so on.

This list of technical tasks should be as comprehensive as possible, In other words, if the team completes all the technical tasks on the list, it should have implemented the associated PBI completely.

That is not to say, however, that the list cannot change after the work is underway. If a new understanding of the business problem comes about during the sprint, the Development Team may add to, change, or delete items from the Sprint Backlog as they see fit.

Just as the Product Backlog is owned by the Product Owner, the Sprint Backlog is owned exclusively by the Development Team. It is their tool, and its sole purpose is to help the team manage itself to accomplish the sprint goal.

The Scrum (Kanban) Board

There are several common ways of representing the Sprint Backlog. The traditional way is by using a *Kanban board*. This can be as simple as taking a whiteboard or other flat surface and dividing it into three columns. Each Sprint Backlog item is written on a "sticky note" and is placed on the board in one of the columns. The first column is labeled "To Do," the second is labeled "In Progress," and the third is labeled "Done." The column in which each sticky note is placed represents the task's current status. At the beginning of each sprint, all the sticky notes should be in the To Do column. At the end of the sprint, they should all (hopefully) be in the Done column.

During the course of the sprint, developers take up tasks to work on from the sprint backlog. If they are using the traditional Kanban board, they pick up one of the sticky notes and move if from the To Do column to the In Progress column. When they finish the task, they move the note to the Done column. Thus, at any given time, a single glance at this "Scrum board" shows a complete picture of what has been finished, what is being worked on, and what has yet to be started.

The Sprint Burndown Chart

Another common way to represent the Sprint Backlog is through a so-called *burndown chart*. This chart is used to show a graphical representation of the *pace* of the work during a sprint.

The chart graphs the Sprint Backlog's status over time. Its vertical axis represents the amount of work left to do at any given time. The horizontal axis represents the number of days in the sprint. The chart is plotted by recording the amount of work left to do on a day-to-day basis. At the beginning of the sprint, the plot mark is made at the top of the scale, indicating that all the work remains to be done. The next day, the plot mark is made one day to the right on the scale and also a little lower, reflecting the work that was finished that day. The amount of remaining work is plotted each day, creating a sloping line that shows progress toward the point in time when there is no work left to do.

The burndown chart often includes an *idealized workflow reference* line. This is a straight line drawn from the beginning of the sprint to the end of it, showing an idealized "smooth" completion of work throughout the course of the sprint. If a sprint contains ten units of work and has a duration of ten days, the burndown chart's idealized reference line would show ten units of work remaining at the beginning, nine units remaining after the first day, eight units remaining after the second day, and so forth.

Useful information can be learned by comparing the idealized workflow reference line on the chart with the actual work completed. If, for instance, the idealized line shows that four units of work should have been completed but the actual line shows that five have been finished, then the team is ahead of schedule. Likewise, if the idealized line shows that three units of work should be left but in fact four of them are not yet finished, the team is behind schedule.

Both the Scrum board view and the burndown chart view of the Sprint Backlog give Development Team members valuable transparency about the status of their work. They need to inspect this transparency regularly to be sure they satisfy the sprint goal to which they agreed with the Product Owner. They do this inspection on a daily basis during a Scrum event called the *Daily Scrum*. The Daily Scrum is a daily opportunity for the Development Team to inspect the transparency provided by the Sprint Backlog and to adapt their work plan to implement the PBIs they agreed to undertake.

Summary

At the beginning of each sprint, the Product Owner and the Development Team negotiate an agreed-on set of PBIs to be delivered. This set of items plus the technical steps needed to implement them make up the Sprint Backlog. The Sprint Backlog is a key artifact because it helps the Development Team keep track of the work it needs to do to fulfill that agreement. It provides the transparency needed for team members to know whether they are on track or not.

The Development Team creates and owns the Sprint Backlog, and can change it any time it sees fit. No one else may do so. In fact, the Development Team need not share or show the Sprint Backlog to anyone outside its own membership. What it contains is, literally, no one else's business.

The Components of Scrum: The Scrum Events

Scrum Events

The Scrum Framework has three main components: *roles, artifacts, and events.* These three components define a way of organizing work to solve complex problems. The roles define *accountabilities,* making clear who is responsible for various kinds of decision making. The artifacts provide *transparency,* providing information in support of the decision-making process. The events provide *forums* within which particular decisions are made.

Scrum is based on the concepts of cross-functional, self-organizing teams using the tools of Empirical Process Control to manage themselves. The five Scrum events are the venues in which the tools of Empirical Process Control are used.

Empirical Process Control relies on the inspection of transparency and adaptation based on the results of that inspection. It is the *scientific method* in disguise. Scientists performs experiments to make certain phenomena clear, observe the results, and adapt their understanding as a result. The Scrum Framework helps its practitioners do work, observe results, and adapt their strategy and tactics to solve the problems they face.

Each of the five Scrum events is an opportunity to inspect transparency and adapt. The five events are as follows:

1. **The Sprint:** During this event, the product is inspected and the Sprint Increment is created and adapted.

2. **The Sprint Planning Meeting:** During this event, the Product Backlog is inspected and the Sprint Backlog is created and adapted.

© Frederik M. Fowler 2019
F. M. Fowler, *Navigating Hybrid Scrum Environments,*
https://doi.org/10.1007/978-1-4842-4164-6_11

3. **The Daily Scrum:** During this event, the Sprint Backlog is inspected and the plan for developing the Sprint Increment is adapted.

4. **The Sprint Review:** During this event, the new version of the product (incorporating all the changes made during the sprint) is inspected and the Product Backlog is adapted.

5. **The Sprint Retrospective:** During this event, the Scrum Team itself is inspected and its way of working together is adapted.

It is very important to realize that these events support decision making by the participants, so they must be used by people who are able and willing to make decisions. The participants in these events must be empowered and must be accountable.

Product Owners must be empowered to make decisions about the Product Backlog and to negotiate about it with the Development Team. The Development Team members must be empowered to choose their own work and to manage themselves to get it done. Both must accept accountability for their own choices.

When the Product Owner and the Development Team are both empowered and accountable, the tools of Empirical Process Control become quite effective for helping them accomplish their goals. The five Scrum events provide a framework for making decisions in a timely and effective way. They empower decision makers to work together to solve problems. They are essential to success when using the Scrum Framework.

When the Product Owner and/or the developers are *not* empowered and do *not* feel accountable, then the tools of Empirical Process Control lose all their effectiveness.

What is the point of a sprint planning meeting when the scope of a sprint has been predetermined by a higher authority? If the Product Owner is constrained by an approved "road map" and cannot change it, what is there to negotiate? If the Development Team is given no choice about what it must work on, what is there for the team members to talk about? Without the ability to make decisions and be accountable for them, the Sprint Planning Meeting is a waste of time

What is the point of a daily scrum if the Development Team feels no accountability for achieving any goals during a sprint? Why should the team get together to make sure it is on track to fulfill a commitment it did not make? If Development Team members make a decision to develop certain features during a sprint, they will find the Daily Scrum to be an essential tool for doing so. If they were given no choice, the Daily Scrum is a pointless exercise.

Many organizations make a serious mistake when trying to implement the Scrum Framework. These organizations try to use Scrum artifacts and events without changing the organization's internal responsibilities. These organizations have plans and designs drawn up by designers, architects, and other subject matter experts. These plans and designs are then given to developers to follow under the direction and control of a PM. The developers are then expected to use the Scrum artifacts and events to follow these plans successfully. It doesn't work.

These tools *must* be used by self-organizing, cross-functional teams. Otherwise, they are worse than useless.

"Time-boxing"

Scrum events all share two important characteristics. They are all opportunities to make decisions and they all have *time-boxes*.

Time-boxing is an important concept in the Scrum Framework. Not only does every Scrum event have a specific purpose, it is also associated with a *reasonable amount of time* within which to serve that purpose.

The longest time-box in the Scrum Framework is the one for the Sprint event. The Sprint may be any appropriate length as long as it is no more than 30 calendar days.

The shortest time-box is the one for the Daily Scrum. The Daily Scrum event should never take more than 15 minutes.

The other events all have time-boxes that are relative to the time-box of the Sprint itself. If a sprint has a time-box of 30 days, then its sprint planning meeting has a time-box of eight hours, the sprint review has a time-box of four hours, and the sprint retrospective has a time-box of three hours. If a sprint is shorter than 30 days, then the time-boxes of these events are correspondingly shorter.

Many people equate these time-boxes to deadlines. They assume that the work of the event must be completed by the end of the time-box *or else*. Many people shut down events arbitrarily when the time-box has been used up.

It is important to realize that time-boxes are not deadlines. They are *reasonable amounts of time* for accomplishing the work at hand. If an event takes longer than the time-box to complete, the answer is not to stop the event. The answer is to *find out why it is taking so long*.

Time-boxes serve the purpose of *transparency*. They make something *clear*. If an event runs past its time-box, the "Scrum Police" should not be sent to arrest the team. Instead, the Scrum Master and the Scrum Team should note the event is taking longer than a reasonable amount of time to complete.

It is an indication that *there is something wrong with the way they are conducting the event.*

The Scrum Master should always take note when time-boxes are being exceeded. They are an "early-warning tripwire," indicating something is wrong.

Something is wrong if the Scrum Team takes longer than eight hours to plan a month-long sprint, more than 15 minutes to understand its daily status, more than four hours to review the results of the sprint's work, or more than three hours to examine itself and understand what happened. There is also something wrong if it takes longer than expected to complete the work the team itself selects to do during a sprint.

If a time-box indicates something is wrong, it is the responsibility of the Scrum Master to figure out what is out of whack. Scrum Masters are accountable for a Scrum Team's proper use of the Scrum Framework. They must teach and coach the Product Owner and the Development Team to conduct the events properly so they stay within the time-boxes.

Scrum Masters should *not* simply stop the event at the end of its time-box. Doing so is similar to turning off a fire alarm after it starts ringing. When the fire alarm rings, it is best to find out what is burning and then put the fire out. Likewise, when an event goes past its time-box, Scrum Masters should find out why, then teach and coach the Scrum Team how to avoid that situation in the future.

Summary

Group decision making can be quite complex if done in an unstructured way. The purpose of the five Scrum events is to provide specific opportunities and venues for making group decisions about specific matters. Each event involves specific decisions that must be made at specific points within the Sprint cycle. This structure is intended to provide focus on the decisions at hand and to help them be made in an efficient way. By encapsulating the decisions within time-boxed events, the amount of time spent on these "overhead" tasks is minimized, freeing up people to spend their time creating the product instead.

The Sprint

The first of the Scrum events is the Sprint. It is unlike the others because it is a "container" event. All the other events happen within the Sprint and its time-box.

More than anything else, the Sprint is a time-box. It divides ongoing work into discrete pieces that are no more than 30 days long. At the beginning of each sprint, there is a sprint planning meeting during which the goals of the sprint's work are agreed on. At the end of the sprint, there is a review of the accomplishments that were made and a discussion of lessons learned. After a sprint ends, a new one begins and the cycle repeats.

The most basic purpose the Sprint serves has to do with the theory of Empirical Process Control. The theory holds that all decisions must be based on measurements rather than predictions. By dividing up work into "iterations," it becomes possible to *measure* the amount of work that can be done over time. If we measure the PBIs completed during a sprint, we can get a measurement of the Scrum team's *velocity*—its ability to get things done. If we measure the team's velocity, we get a statistic we can use for forecasting completion of future work.

Another important purpose of the Sprint is to provide focus for the team. At the beginning of each sprint, there is a meeting during the scope of the sprint is agreed on by all parties. That agreement stays in effect for the duration of the sprint unless all parties agree to change it. This agreement allows the team to focus on the agreed-on priorities and to ignore other demands or requests. Priorities may change drastically by the time the next sprint begins, but for the life of the current sprint, the team focuses exclusively on what was agreed on at the beginning of the sprint.

© Frederik M. Fowler 2019
F. M. Fowler, *Navigating Hybrid Scrum Environments*,
https://doi.org/10.1007/978-1-4842-4164-6_12

The sprint cycle has been likened to a heartbeat for the Scrum Framework. Each cycle takes in a number of PBIs in the beginning and pumps out product features in the end. Too many chaotic scope changes may cause something similar to Ventricular fibrillation, during which the heart tries to beat too fast and can't pump any blood. Too many priorities may mean that none get addressed properly. The focus provided by the Sprint cycle allows the team to focus on producing rather than reacting.

The fact that the Sprint is a *measurement device* leads to a number of important rules for sprints.

Sprints Are Continuous and Contiguous: They Keep on Going and There Is No "in Between"

In order for sprints to be useful in measuring a team's ability to get PBIs implemented, all the work the team does must be included in the measurement. If the team's purpose is to create a product, then *everything it does* is part of that job. *Everything it does* must be measured to figure out the capacity of the team.

A team's velocity is defined as how much of the Product Backlog it implements during a sprint. That information is vital to the Development Team members for forecasting their ability to deliver scope in a sprint. They need to be able to make this forecast to negotiate a sprint scope with the Product Owner.

The team's velocity is also important to the Product Owner. The accuracy of the velocity measurement is vital for making forecasts of future delivery dates of the various features in the Product Backlog.

If sprints were not contiguous (meaning, there is some time in between sprints), then the amount of work needed to create PBIs would not be captured completely within the velocity measurement. Whatever work happened in that "in between" time is hidden and not measured.

For a sprint to be able to measure a team's velocity accurately, it *must* include all the work the team does. All of the team's work must happen within a sprint. There must be no "in between" time.

Sprints Must All Produce "Done" Increments of Product

The Scrum Guide states that the purpose of a sprint is to produce a done increment of product. In other words, whatever is produced during a sprint must be ready to give to a client with no further work required.

In practice, this can be a high threshold to meet. Teams that have not organized themselves very effectively sometimes complete only part of the work needed before the product increment can be given to a client. They point out correctly that they have expended a good deal of effort on the increment even though it is not ready to give to a customer. They ask why that effort "should not "count."

The answer to that question is a different question: How can incomplete work be measured at all?

If someone says the PBI is 90% complete, what does that mean?

"Ninety percent complete" means two things:

1. The work is not done.

2. The amount of work remaining is a guess, and that guess is probably wrong.

It is not possible to measure something that has not happened yet. There is no way to measure the work that is yet to be done and determine that it is 10% of the total. (I have had many instances of a subordinate saying the work was "90% done" after one week and "92% done" after a second week.)

The work product of a sprint *must* be "done" before it can be measurable. That is why *The Scrum Guide* defines "done" as *no further work required*. The work of implementing a PBI can only be measured when there is no further work required to do. Only then can the measurement "count" toward understanding the team's velocity.

Once Agreed To, the Length of the Sprint Should Not Be Changed

The Scrum Guide states that sprints may be no longer than 30 calendar days, but may be shorter. It gives no further restrictions on the lengths of sprints.

In practice, the lengths of sprints are negotiated between Product Owners and Development Teams based on their interests. Product Owners value the transparency of the product that comes at the end of each sprint, and also the ability to change priorities, which comes at the beginning of each new sprint. The Development Team tends to value the stability and focus that exist between the beginning and the end of a sprint. Thus, the Product Owner values "short" sprints and the Development Team values "long sprints." They end up negotiating a compromise at the beginning of the product's life. They stick to this compromise unless there is some drastic change that warrants scrapping the agreement and starting over.

Some people think, mistakenly, that sprints are actually *deadlines* for getting work done. I have heard some Product Owners tell Development Teams they will "hold the sprint open" a few extra days so the team can meet the deadline.

Sprints are not deadlines. They are *measuring tools*. They are needed for teams to measure what they can get done during a fixed period of time.

If a Product Owner "holds open" a sprint so the team can complete everything, this distorts any measurements that might have been made. The Sprint is a yardstick for measuring the amount of results that are produced within it. "Holding the sprint open" is like using a yardstick made from rubber. Stretching it to make things fit results in a lack of accuracy and a lack of understanding about what the team's actual velocity is.

Every Sprint Is Like Every Other Sprint; There Are No "Special" Sprints

Some people give names to certain sprints, implying they are somehow different from other sprints. One such sprint is the so-called *Sprint 0*. Another is the *hardening sprint*.

Sprint 0 (it is claimed) is a different sort of sprint. Its purpose is to "get things ready" so the team can start sprinting effectively afterward. It comes at the very beginning of a project and is in some ways analogous to the idea of Gate 0 in the PMI SDLC framework.

Sprint 0 has the same fundamental structure as any other sprint. It starts with a sprint planning meeting where the Product Backlog is reviewed and a scope is agreed on. The scope is then worked by the team members, who use daily scrum meetings to manage their progress. At the end, there is a sprint review of what has been completed and a sprint retrospective to identify lessons learned. Any item that was not completed is put back into the product backlog and the process repeats.

The so-called Sprint 0 does not differ from any other sprint as far as its structure is concerned. It only differs because of the kinds of goals that are to be met. Measuring the team's ability to get things done does not depend on the kinds of problems they are solving.

The Hardening Sprint is another idea that makes little sense in the context of the Sprint as a measuring tool. It is a sprint in which no new PBIs are attempted. It is just a sprint in which previous work is refactored, shortcuts are reworked, and messy code is "cleaned up." The proponents of hardening sprints recommend that every third or fourth sprint be devoted to these "hardening" activities.

As noted previously, it makes no sense to try to measure work that is not complete. If hardening activities are necessary, does that mean the work done on the hardened items in previous sprints was not complete? Does the velocity recorded from those previous sprints have any accuracy?

Another conundrum is how to measure the impact of the hardening sprint on the team's measured velocity. Clearly the work done on the items in the original sprints was not complete, so efforts during the hardening sprint should be added in to calculate velocity. But which efforts? There is no requirement that a hardening sprint fix only those problems left over from sprints since the previous hardening sprint. There is also no guarantee that all the issues can be fixed in only one hardening sprint. The hardening sprint is just some extra time for the team to work on some things that should have been completed in the first place.

Hardening Sprints ruin a team's ability to measure its velocity. The need for them comes from teams that feel pressure to accomplish more than they are able to accomplish. They take shortcuts to make it appear the work has been completed, but then use the mechanism of the Hardening Sprint to *really* finish the work. (Or not.)

Hardening Sprints cause significant problems in exchange for little (if any) benefit. It is better to finish a PBI completely during its original sprint and then measure the actual velocity achieved by the team. Only then will the statistic make any real sense.

The Definition of "Done"

The requirement to finish every Product Backlog Item during a sprint leads to some interesting questions. When is a PBI finished? When we say it is done, what does *done* mean?

In the Scrum Framework, the word *done* means "ready to give to a customer with no further work required." To determine that no further work is required, it is helpful to understand the kinds of tasks to be performed so that, in the end, the product is ready to give to a customer.

This definition of done can be slippery if not spelled out formally. Everyone tends to view *done* from the point of view of their own contribution rather than from the point of view of the customer. A programmer says the work is done when the programing is complete. A tester says the work is done when the testing is complete. A customer says the work is done when the product can be used by the customer as the customer expects.

Within the Scrum Framework the Development Team is accountable for creating the product. All team members must understand what *done* means from the point of view of the customer, and must accept responsibility for delivering done increments.

The definition of done within the Scrum Framework captures a shared understanding of what it means for an increment to be ready to give to a customer. It often takes the form of a checklist of tasks the development team must blend into its Sprint Backlog.

Using a formal definition of *done* helps make sure completed items at the end of a sprint really do require no further work before they are given to a customer. This makes them measurable and relevant to understanding the team's ability to get things done. This in turn makes progress on working the Product Backlog clearer and more uniform, and—above all—results in a more reliable forecast.

Summary

Sprints are a key element of the Scrum Framework because they provide a way to *measure* the work that is being done. At the end of a specific period of time (in other words, the Sprint time-box), it is possible to see what has been accomplished and thus get an idea of what *can* be accomplished over time.

To be measurable, the work in a sprint must be *done*. In other words, *no further work* is required before the product is given to a customer. A definition of done is often used to identify the standard tasks that need to be performed before the product is ready for customer use.

The amount of *done work* the team can produce in a sprint is called the team's *velocity*. Understanding the team's velocity gives clarity about what can be expected from the team in the future. Applying the measured velocity of a team to the sizes of PBIs in the product backlog gives a way to forecast delivery dates in an empirical way—that is, based on measured facts rather than guesswork.

The Sprint Planning Meeting

Every sprint starts with an event during which the work to be done is agreed on by all parties. A goal for the sprint is set, the scope of the sprint work is agreed on, and a plan for creating the PBIs is formed. This event is known as the *Sprint Planning Meeting*.

Defining the Sprint Goal

The Sprint Goal is a brief, high-level statement of the overall purpose of a sprint. It needs to be short, to the point, and clear. It is the completion of the sentence: We're choosing this work for this sprint because .... It is the answer to the question: Why did we choose these particular PBIs to work on this time?"

Here are some examples of typical sprint goals:

- We wish to create a minimum viable product (MVP) version to use to get beta customer feedback.

- We wish to use this sprint to finish implementing all the back-end APIs.

© Frederik M. Fowler 2019
F. M. Fowler, *Navigating Hybrid Scrum Environments*,
https://doi.org/10.1007/978-1-4842-4164-6_13

- We wish to finish the customer-facing portions of the user interface.

The sprint goal is important for two reasons. First of all, it provides focus and clarity for both the Product Owner and the Development Team when making day-to-day decisions. When developers, for instance, have to choose whether to spend the time necessary to fully "polish" a customer-facing screen, it is important to understand whether the goal is to create an MVP.

The second reason the Sprint Goal is important is that it provides the only way a sprint may be canceled before its time-box expires. *The Scrum Guide* states that the Product Owner may cancel a sprint if the sprint goal becomes "obsolete." In other words, a sprint may be canceled if the point of the sprint no longer has any value. For example, it makes no sense to continue a sprint to create an MVP if one is no longer needed.

The first part of a sprint planning meeting includes a negotiation and agreement about the sprint goal. Agreement must be reached between the Product Owner and the Development Team (with the help of the Scrum Master, if necessary).

Selecting PBIs

After the sprint goal is established, the Product Owner and the developers inspect the Product Backlog. They select and discuss PBIs that will help achieve the sprint goal. The Product Owner provides input about the nature of the problem to be solved and its relative importance from the business's point of view. The Development Team provides input about the relative difficulty of implementing the PBIs from a technical point of view and about any technical dependencies among the items. At the end of the meeting, the Product Owner and the developers will have agreed on a set of items that will deliver the most value possible and will be practical to implement within the constraints of that sprint.

When this agreement is reached it remains unchanged throughout the sprint unless both the Product Owner and the Development Team agree to change it. The Product Owner agrees the work will be limited to the specified PBIs. The developers agree to resolve the PBIs and demonstrate the solutions at the end of the sprint.

Creating the Sprint Backlog

After the scope of the sprint has been agreed on, the Product Owner leaves the Sprint Planning Meeting and the development team members get to work. Their purpose is to create a work plan for implementing the PBIs they have just agreed to undertake. PBIs are descriptions of problems to solve; therefore, the Development Team plans out the solutions as a set of technical tasks to perform. The PBIs and the list of technical tasks necessary to solve them are known as the *Sprint Backlog*.

Understanding the Development Team's Capacity

In order for the Development Team to have a meaningful negotiation with the Product Owner about the scope of a sprint, the developers need to know two related things:

1. What are the sizes of the PBIs? How much team capacity will each one take?

2. What is the team's capacity to do this work? How much work can it take on before the work becomes "too much?"

The theory of Empirical Process Control states that decisions should be based on measurements rather than predictions. Therefore, a Development Team's capacity should be established through measurements. A team should do some work and then measure how much work actually got done to figure out its capacity.

The measured amount of work a team gets done during a sprint is called the team's *velocity*. If a team's velocity is known, then it can be compared to the amount of work represented by the PBIs. Good decisions can then be made by the developers during the Sprint Planning Meeting with regard to what they should attempt to accomplish.

So all that is necessary is for the team to figure out how much work each PBI represents. When it has done that, it can work on those items and measure how much it can get done in a sprint.

Unfortunately, figuring out the size of a PBI is tricky. *The Scrum Guide* mentions a concept called "units of work," but does not define it. To measure something, a *unit of measure* is required. What is the correct unit of measure for the size of a PBI?

Some people maintain that the proper unit of measure to use is *man-hours of effort*. Estimates of the number of man-hours required to implement PBIs can be made and used to gauge how many PBIs will fill a team's capacity.

Unfortunately, using man-hours of effort has several drawbacks:

- Whose man-hours should be used? On any given team, there are different members with different levels of skill. A task that takes an experienced developer only a few hours to perform might take a novice considerably more time to do. Should the size of the PBI depend on which team member will do the work?

- The number of man-hours in a sprint is a fixed quantity. If there are five developers and the sprints are two weeks long, then there are 50 man-days in that sprint. If the sizes of PBIs are expressed in man-hours (or man-days), then the velocity of the team will always be the same. It will always work out to 50 man-days.

- Man-hours are measures of effort. Velocity should be a measure of the team's ability to produce *results* with that effort. Asking "How many man-days worth of work can be accomplished in 50 man-days?" is not very useful (the answer is always 50). Asking "How much *result* can be accomplished in 50 man-days?" is much more useful to know.

As can be seen, the size of PBIs should be expressed in terms of *results* rather than *effort*.

Unfortunately, there is no standardized unit of measure for these results. Man-hours, lines of code, and file size are all measures of effort. Simply counting the PBIs only makes sense if they are all about the same size. If there are big ones and small ones, then counting them does not work.

There is no objective absolute unit of measure that can be used to give sizes to the results produced by a Scrum Team. If we want to measure the length of something, we have yardsticks marked off in inches to do it. If we want to measure the weight of something, we have scales marked off in kilograms to do it. If we want to measure the temperature of something, we have thermometers marked off in degrees to do it. There is no yardstick or scale or thermometer we can use to measure the size of the results produced by a team. There is just no such unit of measure.

Story Points

Although there is no absolute unit of measure relating to the size of a result, we can still measure *relative* sizes to some extent. Let's say that one team of five inexperienced people works hard over the course of a ten-day sprint and produce a pop-up window that says "Hello World." Let's also say that another more experienced team of five developers works hard over the course of a ten-day sprint and produces an entire app. The effort of each team is the same

(50 man-days), but the result is different. We don't know exactly how big the difference is, but we do know the experienced team produced *more result* than the inexperienced team.

Let's say that during the next sprint the inexperienced team was able to produce 25% of a complete app. This is more than they produced before, but still less than the experienced team. Let's also say that a third team produced 50% of an entire app. This is more than the inexperienced team's 25%, but less than the experienced team's 100%.

By comparing results to figure out which is *more* and which is *less*, it is possible to arrange results in a range from smallest to largest. In our example, the range would look like this:

- Smallest: "Hello World" window
- Larger: 25% of an app
- Larger: 50% of an app
- Largest: 100% of an app.

We could then arbitrarily assign a size of 1 point to the smallest result, a size of 20 points to the largest result, and then prorate the sizes of the other results (meaning, 5 points to the 25% result and 10 points for the 50% result). We could then figure out the sizes of other tasks by comparing them to these basic benchmarks.

The arbitrary numbers we assign to these results are called *story points*. After they are calibrated to actual work that has been performed, the Development Team can use them to assign sizes to items in the Product Backlog. The developers can consider an item in the Product Backlog and might, for example, have the following thought process: *Is this bigger than 50% of an app but smaller than 100% of an app? If so, it is between 10 story points and 20 story points. This one feels like a 14-point story.*

It is common for the Development Team to start writing down the technical tasks required to implement the story while they figure out its size.

Product Backlog Refinement

The process of assigning sizes to PBIs and writing down the technical steps needed to implement them is called *product backlog refinement*. Before the Development Team can select items to include in a sprint's scope, the items must be "refined" so that the developers know what they are saying yes to.

Product Backlog Refinement can be done during the Sprint Planning Meeting. The time-box for the Sprint Planning Meeting is the longest one other than the time-box of the Sprint itself. For a month-long sprint, the time-box of the Sprint Planning Meeting is eight hours. A full day is set aside to allow the Scrum Team to agree on a scope and create a Sprint Backlog for getting the scope done.

The time-box is long enough to allow ample time for product backlog refinement activities to occur. Enough PBIs must have been refined before the end of the meeting to make up at least the current sprint's scope. The eight-hour time-box provides ample time for the refining to take place *during the Sprint Planning Meeting* if it hasn't been taken care of beforehand.

It is a good idea to take care of some or all of this refining *before* the Sprint Planning Meeting takes place. *The Scrum Guide* recommends that up to 10% of each sprint be set aside for refining PBIs for future sprints.

It is common practice to schedule two to three product backlog refinement meetings during each sprint. Some people worry that two to three meetings on top of an eight-hour Sprint Planning Meeting seems like quite a bit of time to spend on refinement.

It is important to realize, however, that the amount of refining doesn't necessarily increase. The *timing* of the activity is what gets affected. If the developers and the Product Owner go into a sprint planning meeting in which everyone already understands the PBIs, their size, and the technical tasks they require, there is no reason the Sprint Planning Meeting should take very long at all. The entire event can be over in five minutes if proper preparations are made.

During the Sprint Planning Meeting, the Product Backlog is inspected and the Sprint Backlog is created. If the event is done properly, the Product Owner leaves with a promise from the developers that they will deliver a specific set of PBIs by the end of the sprint. The developers enter into this bargain freely because they chose the PBIs and thus feel accountable for completing them.

Summary

The Sprint Planning Meeting is, in many ways, the heart of the Scrum Framework's sprint cycle. It is where self-organization and cross-functionality matter the most. This is a meeting during which the business side of things and the technical side of things get together to figure out how to move forward.

The Product Owner, representing the business, lays out the needs of the product and identifies the most pressing and important ones. The Development Team, representing the technical side, examines the technical challenges involved in meeting those needs and identifies a specific set of PBIs to accomplish them. The Product Owner and the Development Team *negotiate* over the set of items to be delivered. When agreement is reached, the work of the sprint begins.

The Daily Scrum

When the sprint planning event is complete, several things have happened:

- A sprint goal has been set.
- The Product Owner has a promise from the Development Team that several PBIs will be completed during the sprint.
- The Development Team has produced a plan called the *Sprint Backlog* to get the work done.

The Product Owner has every right to expect the Development Team to keep their collective word and deliver the finished items at the end of the sprint. Because they manage themselves, the developers have to keep track of their work and make sure it gets done.

Usually, developers keep track of the work using a Kanban board, as mentioned earlier. This board shows the current status of all the tasks needed to be performed. In this way, the Kanban board provides *transparency* about the status of the work. The developers need to *inspect* this transparency regularly and adapt their work plan if the inspection shows that some kind of change is warranted.

The Scrum Framework contains an event during which the developers inspect the status of their work and adapt their plan for getting it done (if necessary). This event is called the *daily scrum*. It has two main purposes:

1. To make sure the Development Team understands the status of the work each developer is doing
2. To find out if anyone needs help, then figure out how to provide that help

© Frederik M. Fowler 2019

F. M. Fowler, *Navigating Hybrid Scrum Environments*,
https://doi.org/10.1007/978-1-4842-4164-6_14

The Daily Scrum is a key event for the Development Team because it provides a venue for the team to manage itself. The Daily Scrum is the Development Team's tool to understand its status and to make midcourse corrections. As the work of the sprint progresses, more and more is learned about the work and how to accomplish it. The Daily Scrum provides a way for those learnings to be shared among all team members.

The purpose of the Daily Scrum is to make it possible for the Development Team to keep its promise to the Product Owner at the end of each sprint. Until the sprint is over, the Product Owner has no reason to question the status of the work. For that reason, there is no reason why the Product Owner should attend the Daily Scrum. The only time the status of the work matters to the Product Owner is at the end of a sprint, when the result of the work (in other words, the Sprint Increment) is inspected. Until then, the Product Owner should leave the management of the work to the developers and stay away.

Likewise, the Scrum Master has no direct role in the Daily Scrum. The only responsibility the Scrum Master has is to make sure the daily scrum happens every day and to make sure the developers do it properly. "Doing it properly" means that everyone gets a clear picture of what is going on and the meeting lasts *no more than 15 minutes.*

The time-box for the daily scrum is the shortest of them all. The time-box is always 15 minutes.

The time-box is short for a reason. During a daily scrum, all development activity ceases. All the developers are occupied with the scrum. The sooner they can finish the meeting and get back to work, the better.

The short time-box emphasizes that the Daily Scrum is for *exposing* problems, not solving them. The meeting should bring problems out into the open and make them visible. Plans should then be made to solve them *after the meeting is over.* Trying to solve problems during the meetings take up everyone's time regardless of whether they are involved in the solution. It is better to let everyone else get back to work while only the people involved directly in solving the problem address the issue.

Common Dysfunctions in a Daily Scrum

In many ways, the Daily Scrum is both the simplest Scrum event and also the one that is most often performed poorly. The Scrum Master should watch out for warning signs that indicate the purpose of the Daily Scrum is not being served.

Some warning signs are

- **Poor attendance:** For a Development Team to manage itself properly, everyone must be involved. If some people do not attend the scrum, this may indicate that those people do not feel ownership of the decisions made during the Sprint Planning Meeting. They are "doing their best" but are not accountable for the outcome. They may feel responsible for the work they are doing but not the *results of the work delivered by the team* at the end of the sprint.

  If Scrum Masters notice this behavior, they should examine the way the Sprint Planning Meeting is being held. Do all developers participate in the team's decisions? Do some members feel they are being railroaded by others? Scrum Masters must make sure *everyone feels they have a say* in the sprint planning negotiations; otherwise, it gives those with "no say" license to avoid responsibility.

- **Status reporting:** Sometimes, the Development Team uses the daily scrum to report their status *to the Scrum Master*. When they do so, they are communicating an unspoken message: all their problems are the *responsibility of the Scrum Master to solve*, not the *team's*.

  The Daily Scrum is an opportunity for team members to report their status *to each other*. They must take responsibility themselves to solve the problems they encounter. The Daily Scrum is an opportunity for team members to ask *each other* for help. They should only ask the Scrum Master if they are unable to solve the problem as a team, and the Scrum Master *agrees* they are not capable of solving it without help.

- **The endless daily scrum meeting:** The time-box of the Daily Scrum is 15 minutes, but sometimes the meeting can last much longer. I have joined teams where the daily scrum meeting had been taking two hours to complete. Many people found them to be both boring and frustrating. Clearly, something was wrong.

  The purpose of the Daily Scrum is to provide *transparency* about the work that is underway. Problems that are hampering progress must be brought to light. This should only take a few minutes.

Inexperienced teams often make the mistake of using the daily scrum not just to bring issues out in the open, but also to try to *solve them* as well. It take only a few moments to say "I'm stuck," but it may take hours to find out what is making you "stuck" and figure out how to make you "unstuck." This is what usually causes the daily scrum to last so long.

The correct thing to do is let the daily scrum expose the existence of problems but then let them be solved *outside the meeting*. If someone needs help on something, someone else can offer help during the daily scrum, but the help is provided *after the daily scrum is over*.

When Scrum Masters notice that some developers are trying to solve problems during the daily scrum, they should intervene and ask the developers to save the problem solving until after the daily scrum has brought all the day's other problems to light.

Summary

The Daily Scrum is key part of the development team's toolbox. If it is used properly, it makes success possible for every sprint. It not used properly, development problems can remain hidden until it is too late to fix them in the time allowed for the sprint.

The Sprint Review

At the end of each sprint there is an event to review the work that has been done. This event is called the *Sprint Review* and it is very important for helping Product Owners fulfill their responsibility to deliver value.

Unfortunately, there is a great deal of misunderstanding surrounding the Sprint Review event. Many people believe, mistakenly, that its purpose is to facilitate the formal acceptance of the sprint's work by the Product Owner. This is not the case.

A Common Misconception

This basic misunderstanding leads to a number of erroneous assumptions about the development process itself. Chief among them is that work done during the sprint may not be released to the customer before the sprint is over.

The mistaken view of the Sprint Review holds that it is akin to a "final quality control inspection" of the product before it is "accepted" by the Product Owner. The Development Team demonstrates the results of the work it has performed. All the PBIs accepted by the team must be shown to be in place and working properly. Product Owners may accept or reject them based on how well they conform to the requirements. Any accepted PBIs are then considered releasable to the customers at a time of the Product Owner's choosing. Any rejected items go back on the Product Backlog for reprioritization and rework during a future sprint.

© Frederik M. Fowler 2019
F. M. Fowler, *Navigating Hybrid Scrum Environments*,
https://doi.org/10.1007/978-1-4842-4164-6_15

The True Purpose of the Sprint Review

There are several assumptions about the Scrum Framework that are being made here, and they are not accurate.

First of all, *The Scrum Guide* states that the purpose of a sprint is to "create a done increment of product." It further states that the Sprint Review inspects that done increment. The increment is done if it complies with the definition of *done*. If the increment has satisfied the definition of done, then there is no need for the Product Owner to accept it in a formal way. That done increment needs no such formal inspection.

The second invalid assumption is that a PBI cannot be considered done until the end of a sprint. In fact, the opposite is true. If PBIs are small, they can often be completed (and done) in just a few days. The Product Owner makes a business decision regarding to when to release the work to the customers. If the Product Owner decides to do so, there is no reason why that completed item can't be released *immediately*.

Some people feel the Extreme programming technique of continuous integration, continuous deployment (CICD) is incompatible with Scrum. Once again, the opposite is true. CICD calls for the automation of testing and deployment. Many large software companies deploy their changes to their production environments many times per day. They have automated the process of validating software against the definition of done. These companies can and do use the Scrum Framework.

The Sprint Review is a demonstration and discussion of the Sprint Increment and does not depend on whether portions of that increment *are already in customer hands*. The point is to review *the new version of the product* after the work of the sprint is finished. It is *not relevant* whether some or all of the features and components are in "production."

The purpose of the Sprint Review is not to ask: Is this increment working properly? Rather, the purpose is to note: This is what the product does now. In light of this, what else could it do?

At the beginning of each sprint, the version of the product that contains the changes to which the Product Owner and the developers agree only exists in the imaginations of everyone concerned. At the beginning, the finished product is imaginary. During the sprint, the Development Team changes the product from an imaginary one to a real one. The purpose of the Sprint Review is to inspect that new real product, react to it, and stimulate a discussion of further enhancements.

The primary beneficiary of the Sprint Review is the Product Owner. The Product Owner examines the value the product represents and uses it to stimulate ideas about how the product can be more valuable. These ideas turn into new PBIs. The Product Owner may ask for outside help in examining this new version of the product, and often invites stakeholders and customers to participate in the sprint review and the discussions that ensue.

An Example

An example of an effective sprint review occurred during a software development project that benefitted a not-for-profit organization near San Francisco, California. The organization conducted summer camps for children with cancer and other serious medical conditions. Their grounds contained a large garden full of exotic plants. A donor had given them a number of Apple iPad tablets and they wished to use the tablets as an electronic guide to the garden plants.

During the Sprint Planning Meeting, it was decided to create a database of plant information and display it on the iPad screens. A separate function would allow for the printing of barcode labels for the plants. When the finished product was ready, a user would be able to take a picture of a barcode label with the iPad camera and information about that plant would be displayed.

The Development Team got to work and two weeks later they had something to show. The Product Owner invited representatives of the not-for-profit organization to attend the sprint review.

When the sprint review got underway, the developers showed what they had done. They had not been able to print out the barcode labels yet, but they were able to project a label image on the wall. They then used the iPad camera to read the label, and information about a plant popped up on the iPad screen.

The representatives of the not-for-profit organization were thrilled. "Look at that! It's only been two weeks and something is already working! My goodness."

"And, oh! Look! There is a picture of the plant... Oh. Um, may we have more than one picture?"

The developers and the Product Owner hadn't thought of providing for more than one picture, so they asked why more than one was needed.

The not-for-profit people replied, "Well, we want the child to recognize the plant on the iPad display, so they are sure they are getting information about the right plant. The trouble is, plants look different in the spring than they do in the fall."

At this point the Product Owner interjected, "Oh, so you need *seasonal* pictures—one each for spring, summer, fall, and winter."

The not-for-profit people indicated that was what they wanted.

One of the developers then said, "Okay, I get it. By the way, the iPad has a built-in calendar. Would you like us to figure out what the current season is and then display the associated picture automatically?"

The not-for-profit people asked, "You can do that? Wow!"

Another developer then asked, "Hey, would you like the iPad to talk?"

The not-for-profit people said, "What do you mean?"

The developer went on to explain, "Well, this is an iPad. It has great text-to-speech capabilities. We could put a button on the screen that says 'Talk' and then the iPad could *read the screen out loud*. Would you like us to do that?"

The not-for-profit people then said, "You mean we could use this with kids who are too young to read? We could use this with kids who *can't see? Wow!*"

At the end of the sprint review, the Product Owner added a PBI about a rotating set of four pictures with the default one to be displayed keyed to the calendar date. He also added a PBI about adding a Talk button to the screen that would cause the iPad to read the screen out loud to its user. These two new PBIs greatly added to the value of the final product.

Summary

The Sprint and the Daily Scrum are events during which developers learn about and make decisions about the technical aspects of the product. The Sprint Review is an event during which the Product Owner, stakeholders, and customers learn about and make decisions about the product as it is being conceived and built. This learning process is just as important for the success of the product as it is to the technical expertise of the development team.

The Sprint Retrospective

The final event within a sprint is the Sprint Retrospective. Like all other events within the Scrum Framework, the Sprint Retrospective is an opportunity to inspect transparency and to adapt. Unlike other events during which the Scrum artifacts provide the transparency that is inspected, the Sprint Retrospective is an opportunity for the team to *inspect itself* and adapt the way it works together.

The key to inspection is transparency, and the Sprint Retrospective places a heavy burden on the Scrum Master to encourage and bring out transparency within the team. When facilitated correctly, the Sprint Retrospective does more than anything else to make a Scrum Team effective. More than any other event, this is when Scrum Masters earn their pay.

The format of the Sprint Retrospective is quite simple. The Scrum Team gathers together to discuss things for up to three hours. That's it. There are no artifacts to consider, no decisions to be made, no formal process at all. The Scrum Team members just sit around and talk.

The difference between a bad retrospective and a great one is *what they talk about*. This is where Scrum Masters can make all the difference in the world.

The key to the success of any Scrum event is transparency. The team must inspect transparency to adapt. The challenge with the Sprint Retrospective is that the team must inspect itself. To do this, *the team must be transparent with itself.*

© Frederik M. Fowler 2019
F. M. Fowler, *Navigating Hybrid Scrum Environments*,
https://doi.org/10.1007/978-1-4842-4164-6_16

The job of the Scrum Master is to make the Sprint Retrospective a place where the team *can be transparent.* Transparency of this kind is risky. The Scrum Master must make the Sprint Retrospective a *safe place* where honesty and clarity do not lead to bad consequences.

The Three Questions

For those Scrum Masters who are not very skilled or experienced in facilitating sprint retrospectives, there are several suggested strategies that provide rudimentary help. One of them is the three-questions approach.

The Scrum Guide suggests three questions to be asked of developers during the Daily Scrum:

1. What have you done since the last daily scrum?

2. What do you plan to work on before the next daily scrum?

3. What obstacles or impediments are blocking you?"

Some people use a similar set of three questions for the Sprint Retrospective:

1. What should we start doing?

2. What should we continue doing?

3. What should we stop doing?"

These questions can be useful, but what matters is how comfortable the participants are about talking about "safe" things vs. "risky" things. Usually, safe things are easy to talk about, but represent little value. Risky things, however, represent things of great value but are perceived as dangerous to talk about.

When does one talk only about safe things? One does so when one is among strangers or among people who one does not respect or trust. When is it safe to talk about risky things? When one feels the other people in the room are respectable and trustworthy.

The Scrum Master's task in the Sprint Retrospective is to make it a safe place to talk about risky things. It must be a place where everyone can talk about all of the "elephants in the living room" that everyone knows are there. This requires building trust and mutual respect.

There are two ground rules for successful Sprint Retrospectives:

1. **Sprint retrospectives are closed-door meetings:** The retrospective is a team-building exercise. No one but the team members may be present. If anyone else is in the room, all they will do is dampen any talk of risky things and prevent any discussion of real issues.

2. **No written records of discussions are kept:** The Sprint Retrospective is a place where participants can speak freely without fear of unintended consequences. It should operate under "Vegas rules"—meaning, "What happens in Vegas *stays* in Vegas." What happens in the retrospective *stays* in the retrospective. If some decision or action by the team is to be published after the retrospective is over, the entire Scrum team must agree to do so.

Usually, sprint retrospectives for newly formed teams start out short. Because people haven't learned to trust each other yet, conversation tends to be limited to safe but inconsequential matters.

In this situation, the Scrum Master can start to build trust by steering the conversation toward feel-good items. A Scrum Master should know about everything that occurred during the sprint and can refer to good things, such as, "Hey, Doug! Didn't Sierra really come through for you when you were stuck that day? Didn't she stay late to help you with that tricky problem?" The Scrum Master can then prompt Doug to thank Sierra during the retrospective, which makes both Sierra and Doug feel good, and shows everyone else that the team can recognize and reward people when good things happen.

As the team gets more practice with retrospectives, the Scrum Master can introduce more "edgy" questions, such as: How do you feel about being on this team? Are you proud to be on this team? As team members get more comfortable talking with each other, they can start to address issues in the "risky" category.

Finally there comes a little breakthrough when someone mentions one of the elephants in the room. Often, this is an elephant that is personal. For example, someone might say something like, "Martha, I really admire your skill and talent. I'm not nearly as good as you are, and I know it. I know that everyone else knows it. And I know that you are all laughing at me behind my back. I don't know if I belong on this team."

At this point, the Scrum Master must jump in and make sure there is a positive outcome for the team member who was just dangerously transparent. The Scrum Master can do it by saying something like, "What are you talking about? *Of course* you belong on the team! You don't have the talent that Martha does, but *you never give up.* You're still at it when everyone else has gone home. That has saved us all more than once."

When the team sees that someone can say something as dangerous as that and have a good outcome, the ice is broken and *everyone* starts talking about *all* the things that have been bottled up for so long. That is when the sprint retrospective starts to bump up against the time-box.

After a while, the sprint retrospectives become shorter again because the team members trust and respect each other so much *they no longer need the safety of the retrospective to deal with the elephants in the room.* When this happens, there is no problem the team can't solve. Their productivity takes off and they start showing the 1,500% improvement for which Scrum is famous.

Of all the Scrum Framework events, the Sprint Retrospective *by far* has the most beneficial impact when it is facilitated correctly. It is a shame that so many organizations trying to adopt Scrum do not even bother to hold them.

Summary

The Scrum Framework's success depends on effective teamwork, and no Scrum event is more important for team building than the Sprint Retrospective. The Sprint Retrospective is the part of the Scrum Framework where Scrum Masters really earn their pay. Their ability to make the "retro" a safe place and to facilitate discussions of sensitive subjects can make the difference between mediocre and superior team performance.

If you put a group of people together and give them a task to do, they will initially be focused on each other and their relationships, rather than the problem at hand. The Scrum Master must lead and guide them through the process of working things out. The Sprint Retrospective is the venue the Scrum Master uses to get team members comfortable with each other. After they can work together based on mutual respect and trust, the sky is the limit to what they can do together.

Conclusion

Conclusion

The Scrum Framework is often represented as being very complex, but in reality it is very simple. In many ways, this illusion of complexity is perpetuated by people who understand parts of the framework but not all of it. Things get complex when an organization tries to make Scrum work without embracing it in its entirety. With just one exception (which will be discussed in Appendix A), trying to implement only selective parts of Scrum simply does not work. Doing so makes things worse than they were before.

There are many organizations that try to modify Scrum to "fit the way things are done around here." Those organizations tend to see Scrum as a "methodology" as opposed to being the framework that it is. A methodology is a way of doing things and a framework is a way of organizing things. Organizations who try to "do" Scrum without trying to organize things properly inevitably fail, sometimes with terrible results.

Two of Scrum's components—the Scrum artifacts and the Scrum events—are relatively easy to implement. The idea of a Product Backlog is easy to grasp because it is simply a prioritized list of things for the developers to do. The Sprint Backlog is equally easy to understand. The five Scrum events are easy to comprehend and stage. Most "Scrum in name only" (SINO) organizations use some or all of these tools.

The one part of the Scrum Framework that is only rarely implemented is the most important one by far. Scrum is a framework that organizes things. Above all it organizes *people*. If an entity tries to use the Scrum artifacts and Scrum events in a traditional top-down organizational model, it simply will not work.

© Frederik M. Fowler 2019
F. M. Fowler, *Navigating Hybrid Scrum Environments*,
https://doi.org/10.1007/978-1-4842-4164-6_17

At its heart, the Scrum Framework describes a team of talented people that works together to create value. One team member is responsible for figuring out what kind of product the team should try to create. Another is responsible for making sure the team can work together as a team. The rest of the team figures out how to create that product, then does so. It is as simple as that.

When people are organized into this kind of "self-organizing, cross-functional" team, the Scrum artifacts and events make sense. These tools are specially designed to help self-organizing, cross-functional teams manage themselves and their work. Teams using these tools can and do achieve great things.

Cross-functionality means a team has the ability to create the product with no dependencies on outside resources. Eliminating the possibility of dependencies reduces "friction" so much that many improvements in throughput are common. Unfortunately, many SINO organizations try to overlay Scrum on top of existing team structures, which—most likely—are not cross-functional. The resulting dependency-related issues choke off the possibility of getting much done.

Self-organization means the team takes ownership of delivering results rather than performing tasks. It focuses on solving problems. Usually these smart people get very good at doing so and come up with new and innovative ways of addressing issues in the Product Backlog. Unfortunately, many SINO organizations continue to use centralized decision-making methods to "tell people what to do and how to do it." As they say, "A mind is a terrible thing to waste." Such top-down methods waste the creativity and intelligence of the people actually doing the work. The results are that tasks get completed but problems do not necessarily get solved.

Self-organizing, cross-functional teams seem to be a difficult pill for many organizations to swallow. Likewise, delegating authority to a single person to decide the future of a product is also a stretch.

One of the principals in the Agile Manifesto states:

> Build projects around motivated individuals. Give them the environment and support they need, and trust them to get the job done.[1]

The essential word here is *trust*. The Scrum Team has to work as a team on the basis of mutual respect and trust. The Scrum Team and its parent organization *also* have to work together on the basis of mutual respect and trust.

---

[1]Manifesto for Agile Software Development, principle #5. url:http://agilemanifesto.org.

The parent organization should give its Scrum Teams the environment and support they need. The teams should be trusted to get the job done.

In return, the Scrum Teams must deliver the value the parent organization wants and needs.

This value must be measurable and must be measured. It must be compared to the costs of the team to calculate the return on the parent organization's investment. Ultimately, the ROI of a team is the only real measure of its success.

Doesn't that sound simple?

Scrum for Projects

The Scrum Framework has always emphasized organizing efforts around the creation of products. The definition of Scrum as recorded in *The Scrum Guide* states that the purpose of Scrum is to create products of the highest possible value. The product focus is so central to the Scrum Framework that it identifies an individual (the Product Owner) who is directly accountable for increasing the product's value. There is also an artifact—the Product Backlog—that not only serves to describe the finished product as it is currently envisioned, but also maps out the sequence in which changes and additions to the product will be made.

This "product" focus often presents a barrier to organizations that wish to move from the traditional Software Development Life Cycle (SDLC) framework to the Scrum Framework. In the world of SDLC (aka *waterfall*), the focus is on creating a specific piece of functionality within a fixed budget and timeframe. This work is organized into projects that have a specific deliverable result, budget, and delivery date. Often, this "project" focus simplifies the problem of accounting for the work and recognizing the results as capital assets rather than expenses. These advantages provide powerful incentives for organizations to retain the project focus of their product development efforts.

Often, these organizations attempt to create a "hybrid" form of the Scrum Framework that tries to reap the benefits of Scrum while retaining the SDLC's project-oriented approach. These attempts usually fail for a variety of reasons. As *The Scrum Guide* states: "It is possible to 'pick and choose' among the

© Frederik M. Fowler 2019
F. M. Fowler, *Navigating Hybrid Scrum Environments*,
https://doi.org/10.1007/978-1-4842-4164-6

various parts of Scrum, but the result will not be Scrum." In other words, *The Scrum Guide* invites people to create hybrids, but warns that the benefits of using these hybrids are not guaranteed. Go ahead and modify the framework if you want, but you are doing so at your own risk.

Because so many of these attempts to create project-oriented Scrum hybrids fail, the question arises as to whether it is possible to adapt Scrum for projects at all. Is it possible to use the Scrum Framework effectively if there is no product directly involved? Can Scrum be used to achieve a specific business objective within a specific budget and timeframe?

I've considered this question carefully over many years and many engagements. To my surprise, I believe the answer is yes.

Measuring Value

The Scrum Framework focuses on products for a fairly simple reason. Products have values that can be measured. If you want to know the value of a product, all you have to do is sell it. For both external and internal products, the value of the product is the amount someone is willing to pay for it.

Being able to measure the value of the team's work in this way provides a convenient but powerful way to measure the effectiveness of the Product Owner. Product Owners identify and schedule the work of the development team. Doing so makes them investors, so to speak. They invest the Development Team's resources and time to create a result. Measuring the value of the result (in dollars) makes it possible to compare the value created with the cost of creating it. The primary measure of the effectiveness of product owners is the Return on Investment (ROI) the team achieves.

The value produced by a project is very difficult to measure compared to the value of a product. Often, very elaborate financial justifications are made to get projects approved, but in practice those justifications are rarely measured or proved after the fact. The effects of the project are often mixed together with other effects that have nothing to do with it. It is very hard to isolate and measure the actual impact of a particular project on the overall value of the product being enhanced.

Another difference between projects and products is that, for projects, there are no prioritization decisions to make. The goal or deliverable of the project is fixed at the beginning. The budget is set. The entire project is the result of a prioritization decision made at the beginning by the people who approved the project proposal. So, with no practical way to measure ROI and no real priority decisions to make, what is the need for a Product Owner in a project context?

It turns out there is no real need for the Product Owner role in a pure project context, if all the decisions about priority and scope have been made at the beginning. There is no need for a Product Owner to be accountable for them.

We must not forget, however, that software development represents a complex, adaptive kind of problem. Decisions can be made about a project and its goals before it gets started, but there is no guarantee that those goals cannot change during the course of the work. Things change as more is learned about the project, the work, and the business climate the project is meant to serve. An "owner" is needed during a project to figure out how the project goal (deliverable) should adapt to such changes.

This owner is also useful for breaking the overall project goal into appropriately sized backlog items. In effect, this "project owner" explodes the project goal into a set of PBIs that are refined with the help of the development team. These PBIs are then planned for implementation using the traditional Sprint Planning Meeting mechanism, executed during sprints, and reviewed using the Sprint Review tool. The Development Team measures and records its velocity, which gives the project owner the information needed to forecast completion dates, costs, and related statistics.

There is no role for a product owner in a context where there is no product. There is a role for someone similar to a product owner in a project context, however. This project owner takes the initial requirements, budget, and timeline for the project and constructs a project backlog of items that fulfills those initial requirements. This project owner prioritizes these items to deliver the most value as early in the timeline as possible.

As the project progresses, the project owner notes the velocity of the Development Team and makes forecasts about the final delivery date and cost of the project deliverable. Because the initial estimates for the project were made without any measurements of actual team throughput, any discrepancy between the budgeted cost/delivery date and the forecasted cost/delivery date have to be reconciled. The project owner works with the stakeholders to adjust the project budget, delivery date, and/or scope to match the reality the measurements reveal.

As far as the Development Team goes, there is no real difference in their role in a "project" context as opposed to a "product" context. They work from a backlog managed by the project owner. They engage in refinement activities as usual and negotiate their scope with the project owner during the Sprint Planning Meeting. They should be fully cross-functional and self-organizing as usual. If they operate in a multiteam environment, they should use tools such as the Nexus exoskeleton to identify, mitigate, and manage dependencies.

Summary

Strict Scrum requires a product focus so that the Product Owner can be accountable for the value produced. When the work of development is project focused, the role of the Product Owner must change because there are no obvious decisions the Product Owner makes that affect the value. The overall value delivered by a project is very difficult to measure, so there is little opportunity for a Product Owner to optimize it.

In a project context, however, there are other things to optimize besides value. A project owner can make decisions about the timing of delivered components as well as make decisions to take into account changing business conditions. The project owner can take the business requirements, budget, and timeline established for the project as an indication of the intent of the stakeholders. As long as the need is filled for roughly the amount of money approved and for roughly the amount of time allocated, the project can be considered successful.

The Scrum Framework can be adapted for use in a project-oriented context. To do so, the role of Product Owner needs to be adjusted. Rather than being accountable for maximizing the value of a product, the "project owner" is accountable for serving the intent of the stakeholders, who approved the project scope, budget, and timeline. The project owner assembles and manages a project backlog, and works with the Development Team to refine and prioritize it. The project owner makes decisions when empirical evidence shows that trade-offs between scope, budget, and timeline must be made. The project owner is measured when the project is finished by how well the intent of the stakeholders was actually served.

As the authors of *The Scrum Guide* would point out, adapting Scrum in this way for use in projects is not, in fact, Scrum. It is something else. Whatever its name is, it retains the core principals of self-organization, cross-functionality, and accountability that make the Scrum Framework so successful in a product context. It represents a compromise, but one that preserves the essence of Scrum, rather than crippling it.

Scaled Scrum

The Scrum Guide describes a framework within which a team of 5 to 11 people can organize itself to deliver sophisticated software products quickly and efficiently. Each team needs a Scrum Master, a Product Owner, and three to nine developers to be fully staffed. Experience has shown that such a group of people can be remarkably productive, but the small size of the team does impose limitations on size of the products that can be developed.

A small team of people can accomplish quite a bit. One need only consider the case of the famous Obamacare online application called HealthCare.gov. It was originally developed by a Canadian firm that employed hundreds of developers. After its disastrous debut, the entire application was rewritten from the ground up. After the rewrite, the web site worked quite well and caused no more controversy. It is true that the rewrite took almost a year to accomplish, but the remarkable thing is the size of the team that did it. After hundreds of developers failed to deliver a working product, the web site was reimplemented successfully by a team of just ten people.

Theoretically speaking, a properly organized team of three to nine people should be able to create *any* product. The team members need the support of a good Scrum Master and the guidance of a good Product Owner, but a self-organizing team can figure out how to deliver any kind of functionality needed.

One may try to counter this assertion by saying that three to nine people cannot possibly have all the skills necessary to develop a modern multiplatform system. The answer to this argument is that the self-organizing team need not have expertise in all the relevant technologies *at all times*. The team can adjust its membership as needed, adding expertise in certain technologies and

© Frederik M. Fowler 2019
F. M. Fowler, *Navigating Hybrid Scrum Environments*,
https://doi.org/10.1007/978-1-4842-4164-6

dropping others as required. A single self-organizing team can create any kind of product, no matter the size, simply by taking steps to adjust itself so that it remains fully cross-functional and able to deliver whatever finished work it plans to complete at the end of each sprint.

Why Have More Than One Team Work on a Product?

If a single self-organizing team can create any kind of a product, then why would more than one team ever be needed? The answer is straightforward. A single team can create any product *given enough time*. The *only* reason to employ more than one team to develop a product is to develop it *faster* than can be done with one team alone. A single team can develop a very complex product such as Microsoft's Office suite, but it may take them years to do so. Products such as this one are usually given to a number of teams to work on together. The idea is that if one team can create a product over many months, a number of teams working together can reduce substantially the time required to deliver a finished product.

The idea of having many teams work together to create a product is generally called *scaled scrum*. In theory, scaling up Scrum can shorten the overall development time by allowing different parts of a product to be created in parallel. It is generally recognized that the improvement in throughput cannot increase in a linear fashion. For example, if one team can deliver after six months, two teams cannot necessarily deliver after only three months. Still, the notion that "many hands make for short work" is driving a tendency in the software industry to put dozens (or even hundreds) of teams to work developing a single product.

Scaling the Scrum Framework poses a fundamental challenge. Almost all of Scrum's success depends on having self-organizing teams that are cross-functional. In other words, a Scrum team must manage itself and must be capable of creating the finished product with no outside help. If more than one team is involved, how are they managed? If more than one team is involved, that means (by definition) that neither one can create the finished product without outside help. The Scrum principles of self-organization and cross-functionality are both challenged when more than one team is involved.

There are quite a number of scaled Scrum frameworks that have been developed over the years to try to deal with the problem of organizing multiple teams to create a single product. Some of the more notable ones are DADS (Disciplined Agile Development System), LeSS (Large-Scale Scrum), SAFe (Scaled Agile Framework), Scrum@Scale, and The Nexus. All of these frameworks have their proponents and their detractors, and it is not my intention or purpose to wade into the spirited controversy about which approach is "best." These pages illustrate the importance of dealing with the issues of self-organization and cross-functionality in the context of multiple teams, and describe how one of these frameworks approaches the problems.

Cross-functionality vs. Self-organization

In many ways, the need for cross-functionality and the need for self-organization are in conflict in any Scrum team. Having enough people with enough different skills means a bigger team is a better team. At the same time, the bigger the team, the harder it is for the team members to manage themselves. If the team is too small, it probably doesn't have the ability to create the finished product. If the team is too large, it probably cannot agree on where to go to lunch, let alone make joint decisions about creating the product. In many ways, the guideline of "three to nine developers" in *The Scrum Guide* represents a compromise between these two conflicting needs.

With multiple teams (which really means many more than three to nine developers), the ability for them to self-organize becomes very problematic. The developers *must* manage themselves for the Scrum Framework to be effective. They must choose what they will do and how they will do it, or they will feel no accountability for the result.

Also, if the work of developing the product is divided among more than one team, then the issue of *interteam dependency* is introduced. If team A is working on a function that relies on the work of team B, then team A is dependent on team B to reach its own target. Team A cannot complete its work with "no help from the outside." Team A and team B must coordinate their efforts for both of them to succeed.

The Nexus Framework

In 2015, Ken Schwaber and some of his associates published *The Nexus Guide*, a companion to *The Scrum Guide* meant to provide an "exoskeleton" for extending Scrum principles to three to nine Scrum teams. *The Nexus Guide* (available for download at http://www.Scrum.org) describes a structure that, if used properly, preserves self-organization within the developers and provides a mechanism for minimizing and managing interteam dependencies.

A *Nexus* is a set of three to nine Scrum teams all working to produce a single product. Because only one product is involved, there is only one Product Owner and one Product Backlog. The overall cadence of the sprint cycle is maintained, with each sprint starting with a planning event and ending with a sprint review and a sprint retrospective. There are still daily scrums. The major difference involves the way in which sprints are planned and how sprint retrospectives are handled.

Before sprint planning can take place, the Product Backlog must go through a special product backlog refining process, the purpose of which is to identify potential interteam dependencies in the work to be done. This refinement is done by a special Nexus integration team of developers, working with the Product Owner. Their job is to identify dependent PBIs so they can be grouped together. The idea is that if the items are grouped together, they can be allocated to the same teams and thus avoid as much as possible the need for cross-team coordination.

After the backlog has been refined, the Nexus sprint planning event can take place. Just like the traditional Scrum sprint planning event, the Nexus version is a two-part meeting. The first part consists of a negotiation between the developers and the Product Owner about *what* is to be done. The second part consists of the developers making a plan for *how* to do it.

For all the developers to feel accountable for delivering the result, they must all take part in the negotiation about what is to be done. Therefore, the first part of the Nexus Sprint Planning Meeting is a single meeting that involves all the developers in the Nexus. They negotiate with the Product Owner about the items in the Product Backlog to be done. They agree on a Nexus sprint goal and select a number of PBIs that become the Nexus sprint scope. At that point, the first part of the Nexus sprint planning event comes to a close.

The second part of the Nexus Sprint Planning Meeting should result in sprint backlogs for each of the teams that reflect plans to accomplish all the PBIs selected during part 1 of the meeting. To do this, the entire group of developers then *divides itself into teams* and selects appropriate PBIs on which to work. They select items in a manner that minimizes cross-team dependencies. After the teams are formed and the PBIs are selected, the teams then create their "traditional" sprint backlog.

After the sprint backlogs for each team are created, team members start their development work. They hold their daily scrums and manage themselves to deliver what they have forecast. The Nexus integration team keeps track of interteam dependencies and makes sure they are visible to all concerned. The teams write and integrate their code to produce a single "done" version of the product by the end of the sprint. That version is then reviewed in a single sprint review. The Nexus adapts the Sprint Retrospective event to take into account that there may be lessons learned at both the Nexus level and the individual Scrum team level, but other than that, the Nexus preserves as much of the basic Scrum Framework as possible.

As we can see, the Nexus exoskeleton adapts self-organization for multiple teams by providing different venues and contexts for decisions about *what* is to be done and *how* it will be done. The negotiations with the Product Owner about sprint scope are done with the developers operating as a single group.

Thus, they all have a say in what is to be done and they are all accountable for delivering it.

When it comes to deciding *how* to deliver the agreed-on scope, the developers divide into normal teams of three to nine people and tackle the problems at the team level. Small groups of talented people can solve technical problems much better than large groups. This situation is identical to that of a traditional Scrum Development Team.

In traditional Scrum, the developers negotiate with the Product Owner about the scope they will accept and then make a plan (the Sprint Backlog) to deliver that scope. In the Nexus exoskeleton, the developers also negotiate with the Product Owner and make Sprint Backlogs. The only difference is that, in the Nexus, the developers have the added responsibility of dividing into appropriate teams before they create the Sprint Backlogs.

Summary

Scaling Scrum without crippling it involves adapting the imperatives of cross-functionality and self-organization to a multiteam context while managing the interteam dependencies that are an inevitable result. The Nexus exoskeleton does this by keeping all the developers as one self-organizing body for some purposes, then having them divide into smaller self-organizing bodies for other purposes.

Other frameworks provide other approaches to deal with these issues. I have made no attempt to compare them and have no opinion regarding which approach is the most effective. It is valid, though, to state that the effectiveness of an approach depends on the effectiveness of its way of reconciling the needs of self-organization and cross-functionality in a large-scale product development effort. Self-organization and cross-functionality are the keys to the success of single-team Scrum. Any form of multiteam Scrum must preserve them as much as possible or lose the benefits of the Scrum Framework altogether.

Scrum for the Program and Portfolio Levels

The Scrum Framework as described in *The Scrum Guide* provides a simple and effective way to build individual products. If the products are small enough, they can be developed by a single team of technical people working with the guidance of a Product Owner. If the products are larger, they can be developed by several teams working together using a scaled Scrum framework such as the Nexus. Big or small, the Scrum Framework provides the structure needed to build just about any product.

Most companies do not produce just one single product, though. Only the smallest and/or newest firms rely on just one product for their success. Most commercial organizations search constantly for new kinds of customers and new market niches. They develop and try out new products to address these opportunities.

Organizations that manage their products in a traditional way often group related products into families called *programs*. These programs are then grouped into higher level families called *portfolios*. Top managers (often at the C level) make plans for development activity at the portfolio level, creating

F. M. Fowler, *Navigating Hybrid Scrum Environments*,
https://doi.org/10.1007/978-1-4842-4164-6

initiatives and setting delivery deadlines. These initiatives and deadlines are then decomposed into program-level activities with their own deadlines. These portfolio- and program-level plans are often called *road maps* and they form the basis for the planning of product-level efforts.

The fatal flaw in this approach is that decisions are made based on *predictions* of future results rather than *measurements* of past results. A road map is based on many decisions about things that have not yet happened. It is not possible to judge the accuracy of a road map in advance. The only way to know whether a road map is correct is to work through it and then look at the results.

The Scrum Guide describes product-level planning and decision making very well, but it is silent about higher levels of decision making within an organization. What role is there (if any) for program- and/or portfolio-level management? If an organization uses Empirical Process Control, during which decisions are made based on measured reality, how can people far removed from actual product development make strategic decisions that make sense?

Many people hold different opinions about this question, and at least one popular Scrum Framework (SAFe) attempts to marry traditional portfolio- and program-level management with Scrum teams for the purposes of execution. I believe, however, there is indeed a role for program- and portfolio-level decision making within Scrum, and that those decisions can and should be based on measured results. The definitions of the roles come from the nature of the work of the Product Owner within the Scrum Framework. In other words, the nature and responsibilities of the Product Owner *imply* the nature and work of the *program owner* and the *portfolio owner*.

The Product Owner Is an Investor

As stated in *The Scrum Guide*, the purpose of Scrum is to create "products of the highest possible value." Product Owners are charged with maximizing the value produced by the Scrum Team, and they do this by managing the Product Backlog. The Product Owner's responsibility is to make sure the team is always working on those things that produce the most value. The relative success of Product Owners can be measured based on the amount of value produced.

When Product Owners make decisions about what a team should work on, they are making *investment* decisions. A Scrum Team has a finite capacity; Product Owners control how that capacity is used. When Product Owners make prioritization decisions about items in the Product Backlog, they are deciding how to *invest* team resources to produce the most value.

It is not possible to optimize value unless that value can be measured in an objective way. One of the most important duties of Product Owners is to devise ways to make those measurements in a reliable and unambiguous manner. The easiest way to measure the value of a product is to sell it. For some "internal" products, this approach may not be practical, but nevertheless the value of a product is always what a customer will pay to have it.

Product Owners must always measure the value of the Scrum Teams' work so it can be compared to the cost of producing that value. Because Product Owners are investors, their most important measure of success is the *return* earned on their investments. If Product Owners earn a high rate of return, they are doing a good job. It the rate of return is low (or negative), they are not doing a very good job.

Program and portfolio owners Should Be Investors Too

Product Owners are supposed to get the most value possible out of the Scrum team resources they are given, but *how many resources should they be given?* It makes a difference whether a Product Owner has one team or nine teams to work with. Who should decide how much of a resource should be allocated to develop a given product, and how should that decision be made?

Product Owners are not in a position to make these decisions by themselves. Most Product Owners would want to have as many resources as possible working on their product—to the exclusion of all others. There needs to be another mechanism to make decisions about allocating scarce resources among different products. Here is where the Scrum Framework implies the need for a higher level of decision making than the Product Owner. There needs to be someone, who we will call the *program owner*, who makes decisions about allocating resources to different products, and is accountable for the results of those decisions.

In a "traditional" structure, a program is a family of related products. The program owner oversees a family of related products and the Product Owners accountable for them. The program owner is accountable for maximizing the value of the program (or the *combined value* of all of its products) and makes decisions about allocating resources to the different Product Owners to do so.

Allocating resources among competing products is a complex, adaptive problem that lends itself to a solution involving the Scrum Framework. Program owners may assemble their Product Owners into a kind of Scrum Team and charge them with reviewing allocations and making recommendations for change. They should monitor value delivered and effective ROI, at least at the end of each sprint. The program owner and the Product Owners can form a kind of cross-functional, self-organizing team to solve the problem of how to get the most out of the program resources available.

Similarly, if there are several programs at work within an organization, there needs to be a mechanism for making allocation decisions *among programs*. Groups of programs are called *portfolios*, and the Scrum Framework implies a role of *portfolio owner* to be accountable for these decisions. Portfolio owners may assemble their program owners into a kind of Scrum team to make allocation recommendations. Once again, the success of portfolio owners can be measured by the overall value of the portfolio and the ROI realized by the development of its programs.

It is important to note that, unlike the creation of road maps, these new program- and portfolio-level decision-making processes are all fully empirical. They are all based on measured results rather than predicted ones. It makes sense to invest more resources in a product or program that is producing a high rate of return, and to disinvest resources from ones that are producing a low or negative rate of return. ROI is a statistic that can be measured directly. No guesswork is involved.

Summary

Although *The Scrum Guide* makes no mention of any role higher than Product Owner, it is possible to extrapolate from the duties of product ownership to find the need for program ownership, portfolio ownership, and perhaps higher levels as well. All of these ownership roles are about making investment decisions and earning returns. They differ from each other only by the scope of resources being invested.

I

Index

A

Agile Manifesto, 104
Application program interfaces (APIs), 20
Artifacts, 55
  adaption, 56
  components, 55
  definition, 56
  inspection, 55
  sprint increment, 56
  transparency, 55

B

Behavior-driven development (BDD), 63
Burndown chart, 69
Business requirement documents (BRDs), 35

C

Collocation vs. geographic distribution, 45
Container event, 77
Continuous integration, continuous deployment (CICD), 94

D

Daily scrum, 74
  definition, 89
  dysfunctions, 90
  key event, 90
  purpose of, 90
  timebox, 90

Data base administrators (DBAs), 27

Development team
  accountability, 40
  classifications of, 40
  colocation vs. geographic distribution, 45
  cross-functional, 40
  developer, 39
  differences, 40
  hypothetical, 42
  interaction, 40
  key resource, 42
  responsibilities, 40
  self-organization, 41–43
  team size, 43

E

Events, 73
  accountabilities, 73
  components, 73
  concepts of, 73
  daily scrum, 74
  development team, 74
  organizations, 75
  planning meeting, 73
  retrospective, 74
  review, 74
  timeboxing, 75
  transparency and adapt, 73

F

Forecasting tool, 64

© Frederik M. Fowler 2019
F. M. Fowler, *Navigating Hybrid Scrum Environments*,
https://doi.org/10.1007/978-1-4842-4164-6

G, H, I, J

Gherkins, 63

K, L

Kanban board, 68–69

M

Master role (business)
   definition, 47
   function properly, 48
   impediments, 50
   passive-aggressive, 48
   responsibilities, 48
   servant leadership, 49
   technical decision, 49

Methodology, 103

Military model, 25

N

Nexus framework
   exoskeleton, 113–114
   integration team, 114
   product owner, 114
   sprint planning event, 114

O

Obamacare online application, 111

P

Portfolio and program-level, 117
   decision making, 118
   definition, 117
   fatal flaw, 118
   investor, 119–120
   product-level planning, 118
   product owner (investor), 118

Product backlog, 59
   acceptance criteria, 62–63
   behavior-driven development, 63
   comprehensive release plan, 59
   definition, 59
   forecasting tool, 64
   product owner, 60
   product road map, 59

   status reporting tool, 65
   user story form, 61

Product backlog items (PBIs), 59

Projects
   capital assets, 107
   hybrid form, 107
   product context, 109
   project backlog, 109
   value measurement, 108–109

Q

Quality assurance (QA) team, 20

R

Return on the investment (ROI), 13

Roles of team
   product owner
      characteristics, 32–34
      commitments, 37
      committee, 35
      components, 36
      corporate initiative, 36
      dysfunctions, 34
      e-commerce web site, 34
      product (without), 36
      project manager, 34
      responsibilities, 31
      technical decisions, 32

S

Scaled scrum, 111
   cross-functionality vs.
      self-organization, 113
   definition, 112
   fundamental challenge, 112
   nexus framework, 113–114
   self-organizing team, 112

Scrum
   complex adaptive problems, 7
   components, 103
   definition of, 5
   framework, 4, 6
   friction, 104
   manifesto, 4
   methodologies, 6
   self-evident, 3

self-organization, 104
SINO organizations, 103
software development, 8
step-by-step, 6

Self-organizing team, 28

Servant leadership, 49

Sprint, 77
backlog
burndown chart, 69
Kanban board, 68–69
negotiation, 67
technical tasks, 68
cleaned up, 80
continuous and contiguous, 78
done definition, 81–82
done increment of product, 78
hardening activities, 80–81
increment, 56
lengths of, 79
measuring tools, 80
planning meeting
creation, 84
development team's capacity, 85
disadvantages, 86
goals, 83
product backlog items, 84
refinement, 87
story points, 86
units of work, 85
retrospective, 97
events, 100
feel-good items, 99
questions, 98
rules of, 99
strategies, 98
transparency, 97
review
assumption, 94
development team, 95
final quality control inspection, 93
misconception, 93
not-for-profit, 96
planning meeting, 95
production, 94
purpose of, 94
representatives, 95
XTreme programming technique, 94
theory, 77

Status reporting tool, 65

System development
life cycle (SDLC), 13–14

T, U, V

Team composition, 25
cross-functionality, 27–28
military model, 25
products, 26
self-organization, 28
tools, 26
traditional structures, 25

Team roles, 31

Theoretical base, 9
adaptation, 10
agilists, 12
effective, 11–12
empirical process control, 9
experimental approach, 10
inspection, 10
organizational aspects, 9
scientific method approach, 10
sentinel project, 11
transparency, 10

Theoretical base (artifacts and events), 9

Time-boxing, 75

W, X, Y, Z

Waterfall, 13
assumption, 15
change control process, 15
company's product, 20
consequences of, 20
.CSS file, 18–19
framework, 14
management of, 21
model, 16
plan details, 15
requirement change
requests, 15
software development, 16
studies, 16
system, 17
technical debt, 18, 21
trial and error, 20

Work breakdown schedule (WBS), 14

CPSIA information can be obtained
at www.ICGtesting.com
Printed in the USA
LVHW081810240119
605058LV00009B/13/P